W9-DIJ-071

new small garden

Contemporary principles, planting and practice

new small garden

Contemporary principles, planting and practice

Noel Kingsbury
Photographs by Maayke de Ridder

FRANCES LINCOLN

In memory of Elspeth
Thompson, a dearly beloved
friend, who did so much to
share her happiness through
her love for gardening and
the simple things in life.

Maayke de Ridder

Frances Lincoln Limited
74–77 White Lion Street
Islington N1 9PF

New Small Garden
Copyright © Frances Lincoln
Limited 2016
Text copyright ©
Noel Kingsbury 2016
Photographs copyright © Maayke
de Ridder 2016
First Frances Lincoln
edition 2016

Edited by Zia Allaway
Designed by Becky Clarke Design

All rights reserved. No part of this
publication may be reproduced,
stored in a retrieval system or
transmitted, in any form, or by any
means, electronic, mechanical,
photocopying, recording
or otherwise, without prior
permission in writing from the
publishers or a licence permitting
restricted copying. In the United
Kingdom such licences are issued
by the Copyright Licensing
Agency, Saffron House, 6–10 Kirby
Street, London EC1N 8TS.

A catalogue record for this book is
available from the British Library

ISBN 978-0-7112-3680-6

Printed in China

9 8 7 6 5 4 3 2 1

Quarto is the authority on a wide
range of topics.
Quarto educates, entertains and
enriches the lives of our readers –
enthusiasts and lovers of
hands-on living.

www.QuartoKnows.com

PAGE 1 Disguising the
boundaries of a small garden
will make it appear larger.
DESIGN BY LOUISE VAN DEN AKKER

PAGE 2 Water bounces light
into compact spaces and
creates a rich wildlife habitat.
DESIGN BY DE HEERENHOF

RIGHT This small garden
measures just 25m x 6m (82ft
x 20ft), but the planting layers
have disguised its true size.
DESIGN BY ERWIN STAM

GARY PUBLIC LIBRARY

Contents

Introduction 6

1 Assessing your space
• First things first 10 • Looking for light 14 • Going underground 16

2 Design tricks for small spaces
• Visual illusions 20 • Where does your garden end? 24 • Thinking diagonally 26 • Less isn't always more 27 • Filling the space effectively 28 • Interesting the feet 30 • Injecting detail 31 • Introducing focal points 32 • Taking the gaze up 34 • Combining functional spaces 35 • Including sensory experiences 36 • Linking the house and garden 37 • Case study 38

3 Layering with plants
• Nature's way 42 • Structural plants 44 • Sculpting with woody plants 48 • Herbaceous and short-lived plants 54 • The lawn 60 • Visual plant layering 62 • How to layer with plants 64 • Naturalistic plant layering 66 • Case study 72

4 Plants for small gardens
• Choosing plants 78 • Seasonal changes 80 • Plants with staying power 82 • Late-season blooms 84 • Two-season plants 86 • Focus on foliage 88 • Using colourful leaves 90 • Choosing evergreens 94 • Including structure 96 • Designing with grasses 101 • Introducing scent 102 • Cultivating the exotic look 104 • Case study 106

5 Vertical planting
• Climbing high 110 • How plants climb 112 • Right climber, right place 114 • Trailing and flowing effects 118

6 Mini wildlife havens
• Small sanctuaries 122 • Nurturing environments 124 • Providing water 126 • Selecting plants for wildlife 128 • Wildlife-friendly garden features 132 • Case study 134

7 Sustainable small spaces
• Designs for compact eco-friendly gardens 138 • Managing water in urban gardens 140 • Planning and planting a mini rain garden 142 • Making hard surfaces porous 146 • Introducing recycled and reused materials 148

8 Containers for small plots
• Creative displays for containers 154 • Choosing containers 156 • Top container design tips 160 • Container care 162 • Choosing plants for pots 166 • Case study 168

9 Making space for food
• Creating a tiny fruit and vegetable plot 172 • Types of vegetable 174 • Types of fruit 176 • The home vegetable-growing revolution 178 • Choosing a productive site 180 • Protecting crops in tiny plots 182 • Case study 184

Plant selector
• Trees 188 • Shrubs 188 • Sub-shrubs 192 • Perennials 193 • Grasses 198 • Climbers 200 • Bulbs 201

• Designers' and Garden Contacts 202
• Index 203
• Acknowledgements 208

Introduction

Most people have small gardens, and with populations rising, particularly in urban areas, the number is sure to increase further. Those with limited outdoor space also tend to be younger, with less gardening experience, and are therefore often also beginners.

This is a book about making the most of your small garden, with a particular focus on the plants, aimed at both novice gardeners and those with more experience. Plants are absolutely central to the whole idea of the garden, yet they can often be the least expensive element, and here I offer a guide to selecting and combining them to create the best effects.

Too many books on small gardens feature lots of pictures of hard landscaping or designs at flower shows where no expense has been spared. This book focuses on 'real' gardens, with case studies of real people with real problems to solve. Most featured are under 100 square metres (328 square feet) – a few are slightly larger, some very much smaller – but all work on similar principles, which you can follow whatever your plot size. Many of the gardens are in the Netherlands, where the country's high population density means that most people have limited outdoor space and Dutch designers have devised practical, imaginative solutions to transform them into green oases.

Demystifying planting design

Growing plants is an immensely life-affirming activity, but choosing those appropriate to the site and space available requires knowledge and skill, to say nothing

of putting them together to make combinations that work and look good. Selecting the right plants for your particular site is a wonderfully enriching but sometimes frustrating process, much of it learned by trial and error. To demystify the process, this book clearly explains the basic principles of how plants grow and work together, and includes the tools to help you make decisions about both the design and the planting of your small space. I have also included a wide range of plant choices suitable for small gardens throughout the book and in the Plant Selector on pp186–201.

Gardens serve many purposes: as outdoor rooms, as places to grow plants for both pleasure and food, and, increasingly, as mini nature reserves. I aim to introduce you to all of these and help you to enrich your lives in the process.

Noel Kingsbury

LEFT Tightly packed borders imitate the way plants grow in nature. Sheltered by a pear tree, bright pink *Lychnis coronaria*, opium poppies (*Papaver somniferum*), foxgloves (*Digitalis purpurea*) and the catmint, *Nepeta* 'Six Hills Giant' create layers of planting that produce a thickly woven tapestry effect.
DESIGN BY JOKE & HENK CIJSOUW

ABOVE RIGHT This tiny town garden is tucked between other houses in London, yet the prolific planting disguises its boundaries and makes it feel like a much larger space.
DESIGN BY STEPHEN SMITH & JONATHAN McKEE

1

Assessing your space

First things first

When planning the style and planting for a small garden, first consider what you want to use it for and take a close look at your soil and the amount of light your garden receives, as these factors will affect your plant choices.

How gardens function

Before you begin designing your garden, assess its various functions and what you want to use it for – make a list and prioritise your needs in order of importance. A garden's ability to multi-task is governed by a number of factors. It is easier to make the space perform several functions in a large garden, or one with a complex shape, but in a small space we have to think more carefully about how to make it work, both visually and practically. Aspect – the way the garden faces and, crucially, how much sun it gets – together with soil type may also govern how well your garden fulfils its purpose.

First, let's look at what we typically ask of gardens. A garden may be a place to grow plants for pleasure; raise crops; exercise a pet; provide space for children to play; sit and relax; and eat and entertain. In addition, it may have to accommodate storage space for bicycles, or barbecue equipment and furniture.

When thinking about function, it helps to consider the main point from which the garden will be seen. In most cases this will be the house, but also bear in mind the place from which the garden will be viewed while it is being used. The most common uses are eating and relaxing in the sun, and ideally those eating or relaxing will look up and see a beautiful garden. Most of us will, realistically,

LEFT This leafy corner of a town garden shows just how much a plant-lover can squeeze into their small space: annuals, climbers, shrubs, perennials and a lawn. DESIGN BY CAROLIEN BARKMAN

TOP RIGHT Cities are often warm, allowing plants such as this tender banana (*Musa basjoo*) to form part of the plant-based screening. DESIGN BY ZAKI AND RUTH ELIA

CENTRE RIGHT Shelves, which are normally thought of as domestic fittings, can be useful in small gardens,

raising plants up nearer to the light and providing storage space below. DESIGN BY DE HEERENHOF

BOTTOM RIGHT Think ahead when buying a playhouse for children and look for one that can serve as a shed when your little ones grow up. DESIGN BY ROBERT BROEKEMA

PREVIOUS PAGE Grasses, corten steel containers and the distinctive shrub *Aralia elata* lend a contemporary look to a London rooftop garden. DESIGN BY KWEKERIJ VAN NATURE

want to dine or sit close to the property, so the viewing point will often be the same as that from the house, but the shape, size and aspect may mean that this is not necessarily the best option. Other areas of the garden may receive more sun or offer shade beneath a mature tree, for example, so look at these carefully at the planning stage and assess their suitability.

Size matters

You will also need to work out how much space you actually have, and be realistic about what you will be able to do with it. Most of the functions mentioned above require a flat, and more or less level, usable surface, and it is this space that will dominate your design. You may also want to install a hard surface, such as paving or decking, or a lawn. Although lawns are often a default feature for gardens, at least in temperate climates, they are not always the best landscaping solution for a small space, so think carefully before laying one (see pp.60–61).

Many plants require a horizontal area to grow well, but remember that you can also use the vertical space. A small garden may, in fact, have a larger vertical surface area than ground space. How much do you have and what is it – a wall, fence or hedge? Vertical space can be adorned with climbing plants (see Chapter 5; pp.108–119) or use it to add storage with cupboard-like structures. The boundaries can also visually enhance your small garden, either by using them to display artworks or by painting or staining the surfaces.

Shaping up your space

The shape of your garden can influence its design and function. Square gardens provide fewer opportunities for visual interest than rectangular plots, as everything tends to be seen at once. A rectangular garden, on the other hand, offers the chance to create more than one zone, particularly if it stretches away from the house, increasing the number of functions and visual experiences you can incorporate. However, a very narrow rectangular space can look like a corridor, and its use may be more limited.

'Shallow' plots, where the rear boundary runs close to the house, are also difficult to design, as they offer little sense of the garden being separate from the house. In these cases, the viewing point may be best

> "A rectangular garden offers the chance to include more than one zone, increasing the number of functions and visual experiences."

placed in one corner, so that you look at the garden along a diagonal axis, even though this may take both viewpoint and axis away from the house.

Gardens with more complex shapes, such as those with distinct 'limbs', are a boon, as each section can be developed separately, even if one of those functions is only to hide a compost bin or a shed.

LEFT In small gardens, choose trees with airy canopies and upright growth, or remove the lower branches to allow more light through.
DESIGN BY TOM DE WITTE

RIGHT Planting plenty of greenery immediately outside wide patio doors helps to integrate house and garden, while also softening the hard landscaping and boundary walls.
DESIGN BY KWEKERIJ VAN NATURE

BELOW Multifunctional features such as this rustic woven fence, which hides a messy area and also supports climbing plants, and pots that double as lights, are great design solutions for tiny spaces.
DESIGN BY KRISTOF VAN DEN BOUWHUYSEN

Looking for light

Professional designers always assess a garden's 'aspect' before creating a plan. This refers to the direction the garden or, more precisely, the side of the house faces, and dictates how much sun your plot will receive, and where and when it falls, depending on whether the garden looks north, south, east or west.

For most of us, the ideal aspect is a south-facing garden, which means that for most of the day you step out into the light, although during warm summers this may not be such an attractive feature. The end of the garden will face away from the sun and be shaded, providing an ideal place for a compost heap, an unkempt 'wildlife corner', and other bits and pieces.

The next best aspect is a west-facing garden, which means that the side of the house receives afternoon and evening sun – ideal for entertaining. East-facing plots offer a great breakfast venue, if not a good place for cocktails or a barbecue in the setting sun. In gardens that face north, away from the sun, you will step out into shade, but if long enough, there is a good chance that the opposite end of the garden will be in the sun and provide the ideal main viewing point (see pp.11–12). This may be less convenient and mean that you will be looking back through the garden to the house, but it could still be the most attractive option.

Shady situations

In some situations, mostly urban ones, the whole garden may be shaded by trees or buildings. A shaded garden is not necessarily a bad thing for plants (plenty flourish in shade) but it is not so pleasant for humans, at least in cool climates, although in warm areas it may well be a boon. A shaded garden will need all the extra light it can get, so hard materials should be pale in colour, while white or pastel-coloured walls and fences will help brighten it up too.

The position of the sun will change throughout the year, and although it is possible to calculate the angle at which sunlight will hit the garden during different seasons, it's easier just to observe it. In fact, you only need to take notes for six months of the year – from one solstice to another (i.e. midsummer's day to midwinter) – to assess how much light will fall on your garden during the different seasons. This is because the sun's angle will be the same 90 days before the solstice as 90 days after. The key factor for most people is knowing the spot that receives the last rays of sun on summer evenings, which will be the ideal main viewing point and place to site a barbecue and dining table.

LEFT A south-facing aspect can be a boon in a small garden, allowing plants, such as this *Cornus kousa* 'Milky Way' to thrive, but it may prove too hot in summer. The awning offers a temporary lightweight shade, making the sitting area more comfortable. DESIGN BY GARDENS OF APPELTERN

RIGHT Blue *Galega orientalis* and the purple heads of *Allium hollandicum* fill a small, partly shaded border in early summer. The yew, *Taxus baccata* 'Fastigiata Aurea', is amenable to sun or shade. DESIGN BY HELEN DILLON

Going underground

As well as considering the sun your garden receives, the other crucial factor to take into account when designing a garden is the soil type. Even in a small space, there may be differences in soil quality between one area and another, especially in gardens where building work has taken place. In an ideal world you will have a good quality loam, which is neither too wet nor too dry, but in reality you may have one of the following soils:

- **Very dry soil** Usually the result of a very free-draining sandy soil or one full of building rubble, dry soil can also be caused by tree roots sucking out moisture or buildings casting a 'rain shadow', making adjacent gardens very dry. You can try adding plenty of organic matter (see below) or, if the soil is very poor quality or shallow, construct raised beds and fill them with imported soil. Selecting drought-tolerant plants should be your priority.

- **Poorly drained soil** Water which stands in puddles for days on end indicates poor drainage. If the soil is compacted, it may be possible to improve drainage by breaking through the impervious layer, but in a small space, it is often difficult to find anywhere for water to drain. Accepting the inevitable and growing wetland plants is one solution, or use raised beds to bring the plants' roots above the water level.

- **Poor acid soil** This can be recognised by observing the type of plants that are growing in neighbouring gardens and the surrounding area. Very sandy, acid soils may limit your plant choices, but they have their own specialist flora which is very attractive and has the advantage of being mostly evergreen. Examples of acid-lovers include birch trees, rhododendrons, camellias and heathers.

- **Poor dry limestone soil** Such soils may be natural, or the result of buried rubble or building foundations. They are typically dry, while the high lime content also makes them very alkaline and often renders soil nutrients insoluble. A relatively small palette of plants will thrive on these soils.

CHECK YOUR SOIL'S ACIDITY

A basic soil test kit (below) will measure your soil's acidity (pH). Acid soil (below pH 7) tends to be infertile, and many plants grow poorly on it, although some beautiful types will actually thrive here. In fact, because a range of highly sought-after spring-flowering shrubs, such as rhododendrons and camellias, prefer acid soils, many gardeners are happy with these conditions. However, vegetable growers or rose-lovers would have no success. Neutral or very slightly acid (pH 6.5–7) soil is the optimum for fertility and supports a wide range of plants. Moderately alkaline soils (pH above 7) can be fertile, but very alkaline soils (pH 8) often suffer from 'nutrient lock-up' and low fertility.

Improving your soil

Although you can help to improve poor soils, choosing plants that will flourish naturally in your conditions can save an awful lot of hard work and expense. Much depends on what you want to grow. Vegetables and fruit need good, fertile soil, as do some annuals, so if you want a bumper harvest or annual bedding displays then, by all means, buy in lots of composted green waste (or make your own), and add fertiliser to the soil.

Composted organic material will help improve a wide variety of poor soils, but rather than digging it in, spread a thick layer over the surface as a mulch and leave the worms to pull it down into the lower depths. This method increases fertility, releasing nutrients over many months, and also improves the soil structure.

Plants for very dry soil

Plants that thrive in dry soils tend to hail from hot climates, such as the Mediterranean regions. Many have silvery or furry leaves, which help the plants to retain moisture, either by reflecting sunlight or trapping dew droplets between the hairs on the foliage. These plants usually prefer full sun.

PLANTS FOR VERY DRY SOIL

- *Ceanothus* species
- *Cistus* species
- *Eryngium bourgatii*
- *Geranium sanguineum*
- *Iris* – bearded types
- *Lavandula* species (pictured)
- *Liatris spicata*
- *Nepeta* x *faassenii*
- *Perovskia atriplicifolia*
- *Pulsatilla vulgaris*
- *Sedum spectabile*
- *Thymus* species

Plants for poor drainage

Plants that flourish on wet soils tend to grow large and lush, with tall stems and spreading leaves. Most do not like to be wet all the time, preferring drier conditions in summer. They also tend to grow vigorously and over-enthusiastic growth will need editing out to prevent one species from dominating.

PLANTS FOR SOIL WITH POOR DRAINAGE

- *Acorus gramineus*
- *Alchemilla mollis*
- *Amelanchier* species
- *Astilbe* species
- *Caltha palustris*
- *Filipendula* species
- *Hemerocallis* species
- *Hosta* species (pictured)
- *Lythrum salicaria*
- *Mentha* species
- *Salix* species
- *Sanguisorba* species
- *Trollius* species

Plants for poor acid soil

Most plants do not grow well on poor acid soils, but there are some that relish these conditions. Many are members of the heather/rhododendron family, which, in fact, grow poorly in 'better' conditions. Most are spring- or early summer flowering, but a few flower later, and they include some grasses for winter interest.

PLANTS FOR POOR ACID SOIL

- *Calluna vulgaris*
- *Camellia* species
- *Deschampsia cespitosa*
- *Erica* species
- *Hydrangea serrata*
- *Molinia caerulea*
- *Pieris* species
- *Rhododendron* species (pictured)
- *Sesleria* species
- *Vaccinium* species

Plants for limestone soil

The majority of species that grow well on these nutrient-poor soils flower profusely in early summer, but then become dormant later in the season as the soil dries out. Some, such as varieties of *Nepeta* and *Salvia nemorosa*, then make a recovery later in the autumn as the rains return and conditions improve again.

PLANTS FOR LIMESTONE SOIL

- *Allium* – smaller species (pictured)
- *Armeria* species
- *Campanula* – smaller species
- *Dianthus* species
- *Euphorbia cyparissias*
- *Nepeta* – low-growing species
- *Origanum* species
- *Salvia nemorosa, S.* x *superba, S.* x *sylvestris*
- *Thymus* species
- *Veronica austriaca*

2

Design tricks for small spaces

Visual illusions

Designers employ a number of visual tricks to deceive the eye and make small gardens appear larger. Some may at first seem counter-intuitive, such as using large plants and blocking the view through the space.

Dividing lines

"You must not see everything at once." This is something almost every garden designer will tell you during a conversation about gardens, large or small. They will also very often say that a garden should be a journey. If you can see everything at once, from one vantage point, then you have seen the garden . . . that's it . . . done. If, however, you catch glimpses of places that suggest there is more beyond, then you have created a reason to get up and explore, and the journey has begun.

British designer Annie Guilfoyle, who created some of the gardens in this book, suggests dividing up the space, if possible, to make the garden more intriguing. Carving up a small garden to form physically different areas is one of the most effective ways of making it seem larger, but if your plot is not big enough, then the next best thing is to include a couple of extra places to stop, such as a bench or seat. These allow you to see the garden from different angles and provide multiple viewpoints, which will also help to visually enlarge the space.

Although you may not be able to subdivide a really tiny garden, it is nearly always possible to make people *think* there is more to look at. One design trick, employed by Annie and others, is to include a false door, making the garden look as though it goes on further.

LEFT Planting in this compact 'pipeline' garden helps disguise the boundaries. The bold *Geranium* 'Anne Thomson' on the left and grass *Hakonechloa macra*, opposite, also help to divide the space.
DESIGN BY TOM DE WITTE

TOP RIGHT A 'dummy' door appears to lead to another garden, and even once you know it's a trick, suggests this small urban space has greater depths.
DESIGN BY JOANNE BERNSTEIN

CENTRE RIGHT Clipped hornbeam hedges mask the perimeters of this compact garden, while the dramatic *Molopospermum peloponnesiacum*, holds the focus in the foreground.
DESIGN BY TOM DE WITTE

BOTTOM RIGHT Varying the materials on the ground makes small spaces more interesting; the simple geometric shapes also create a restful atmosphere.
DESIGN BY LUC ENGELHARD

PREVIOUS PAGE The boundaries around the dining area in this small garden are cleverly disguised, making it feel larger.
DESIGN BY ROBERT BROEKEMA

Another effective trick is to install a mirror, and then conceal its edge, perhaps with plants; it is always fascinating to watch a visitor who peers, walks towards the mirror and then stops, realising they have been fooled. Mirrors also introduce more light and help to open up a space, and, together with a false door, they can help create the fantasy that the garden is not only bigger but also has secrets to hide, that another world exists in the imagination.

Mystery tour

Some of the best garden designers make, or suggest, different ways of arriving at the same point. Dutch designer Tom de Witte often uses this device to make a space seem bigger, and says that by creating different routes you also double the visual interest and allow plants and features to be viewed from different angles.

Another idea is to use coulisses to subdivide a small space. A coulisse is a flat piece of scenery at the side of the stage in a theatre, or the gap between the scenery panels where actors make entrances and exits. In a garden context, it could be a short run of hedging, an upright-growing plant or a narrow trellis panel just wide enough to hide behind. Masking what is beyond it creates a little sense of mystery, just enough to prompt the visitor to ask, "What's there?" Or, if wide enough, it can provide space for a seat, offering a completely different, and more tightly framed, view of the garden.

A coulisse can also help to break up the design, but it does not always have to be set to one side. A bold garden-maker may put some sort of screen right in the middle of the garden, begging the question, "What is behind?" Screens can be solid or, better still, semi-transparent. Fencing with gaps or narrow-stemmed plants partially obscuring, but not completely blocking, views help to create ambiguity and heighten mystery. A screen that partly shields a significant feature, such as a pool, dining area, showy shrub or distant view, is particularly effective, prompting the onlooker to want to explore further.

"A screen that partly shields a feature, such as a pool, dining area, or showy shrub, is particularly effective, prompting the onlooker to want to explore further."

LEFT Where there is enough room, dividing a small garden can do much to increase the sense of space; two routes to one destination also allows you to view the features from different perspectives.
DESIGN BY MARIANNE BLAAUWBOER

ABOVE RIGHT This long thin town garden is broken up by planting that comes in from the sides to create depth and diversity. Climbers provide height and soften the impact of the surrounding walls.
DESIGN BY CAROLIEN BARKMAN

FAR RIGHT A wooden screen hides an oil tank, while a blue-leaved hosta fills a space in a narrow border. Hostas are good choices for drawing the eye and creating a sense of mass in a planting scheme.
DESIGN BY KATE GOULD

RIGHT What we read as a gate may, in fact, be a fence bordering a neighbour's garden. Openings with structures that look like they permit access always create the sense that the garden extends further.
DESIGN BY LYDIA GUNNING

Where does your garden end?

If a visitor, standing on the terrace or at the back door, asks this question, you have triumphed. If it is unclear how large the garden is, then it is no longer a 'small garden', at least psychologically. The surroundings can also be perceived as part of the garden: your plot is not just what is legally and physically yours, but also what you can include visually. Think of this additional space as a 'virtual garden'. Blurring the boundaries is key to the Japanese concept of *shakkei* or 'borrowed landscape' and the easiest way to achieve this is with foliage – small trees and shrubs, climbers, evergreens and bamboos – that fills the space. But blurring the boundaries is not necessarily about hiding your fence or wall; very often, simply breaking up boundary lines is all that is needed. Trees and shrubs that poke above your fence and merge with trees behind them are

"Your plot is not just what is legally and physically yours, but also what you can include visually."

LEFT Trees on either side of the hedge at the bottom of this deceptively small garden help to confuse our perception of where it ends. The pool's longitudinal thrust emphasises the length of the space too and creates a more expansive atmosphere.
DESIGN BY ROBERT BROEKEMA

ABOVE LEFT An inward-looking garden, here achieved with masses of exotic foliage around the outside coupled with distinctive tiling, keeps the eye looking towards the centre. Much of the foliage is evergreen, creating this screening effect year round.
DESIGN BY ZAKI & RUTH ELIA

ABOVE RIGHT The water at the bottom of this garden may be a canal, but it could be (in the imagination at least) a lake – your lake. Changes in the paving design and steps at different angles subtly engage the attention as you walk to the water's edge.
DESIGN BY LUC ENGELHARD

effective, or use a large shrub or tree that blends with neighbouring greenery, together with a path on one side of it, suggesting that the route continues through.

Long thin gardens, known as 'pipeline' gardens in the Netherlands, may at first feel constraining, but they do offer the opportunity to design a series of sub-gardens, set one behind the other, which together create a journey. It is so much easier to blur the end of a long, thin garden than a wide shallow area, where the boundary is right in front of you, but even here, you can disguise the end. Annie Guilfoyle suggests hiding the boundaries with large masses, such as leafy plants and hedges, or man-made structures like pergolas.

Thinking diagonally – the bishop's move

Just as a bishop's move in chess can be a dramatic sweep that catches an opponent unawares, so can thinking diagonally in a garden. The classical tradition which underpins all Western ideas about space can be very unhelpful in thinking creatively about small spaces, as it focuses on axes at right angles to each other and focal points. More inventive ways of looking are needed, and the diagonal can be particularly useful, since it creates the longest sight-line in a rectangular space. The shorter sight-lines on either side of the midpoint of that diagonal will also be longer than those in a space divided by right angles.

Designer Annie Guilfoyle often sets the whole garden plan on a diagonal, not only because it creates the longest lines in the garden but also because it makes fat triangles on either side for planting, rather than narrow borders around the perimeter. This last point is important as it creates deep planting beds; so many gardens have a central lawn with a mean little strip around the sides for plants that is rarely wide enough for the layers needed to provide year-round interest.

BELOW At ground level the diagonal makes the longest possible axis in this small town garden. From a first floor window, the effect is very different to that of most gardens, lending a dynamic touch.
DESIGN BY STEPHEN SMITH & JONATHAN MCKEE

ABOVE The diagonal layout of the paving slabs in this courtyard garden helps to make the space feel larger, while the small tree and hedge in the centre hide the back of the garden.
DESIGN BY KWEKERIJ VAN NATURE

Less isn't always more

One of the most widely touted design maxims is 'less is more'. Minimalism, or paring down to bare, ascetic essentials, has been fashionable for a long time, but countering this trend has been a move towards ornament, decoration, complexity, and an evocation of the baroque or celebration of kitsch. The amount of ornament and visual richness you include is a matter of taste, but you do not have to choose one style or the other, as it is possible to create different levels of 'less' and 'more'.

Designer Tom de Witte advises gardeners, whatever their preference, to repeat materials to lend a sense of continuity and connection. Visual unity is particularly important in complex or awkward spaces that comprise different areas, which can be linked with one element common to all. This may be a hard surface, such as paving, or a long-season plant that appears in each segment. Unifying several small spaces visually may seem like contradicting the advice above to subdivide, but this is not necessarily so, as the whole can be perceived as one, but with different areas designed with their own subtle twist.

Carolien Barkman, a Dutch garden designer known for her inventive solutions for compact city gardens, suggests using paving and a uniform wall colour to link different areas of a garden. She also includes a group of specified plants throughout the whole space but changes the style of planting in each area, creating both unity *and* differentiation – less *and* more.

Reducing the visual complexity of a design conveys a sense of simplicity and calmness, which most of us want from our gardens, and a unifying material or plant will help to achieve this. However, it is best to use this feature on a macro level, linking the garden as a whole, while ensuring that unifying elements do not dominate to the exclusion of everything else, which could make your design look boring. Detail on a micro level, with plenty to look at – or indeed smell, feel and hear – will provide additional interest on the journey through the space.

FEATURES THAT LEND VISUAL UNITY

- A ground surface material running through the whole area: paving, lawn, decking.
- The same treatment for as much of the boundary as possible.
- Repeating a distinctive permanent element; for example, a strong colour, clear plant shape, or sculptural feature.
- Repeating the same short-season plant, such as snowdrops in spring, self-sowing English marigolds (*Calendula officinalis*) in summer, and a small feathery grass, such as *Stipa tenuissima*, for autumn and winter.

> "Reducing the visual complexity of a small garden design conveys a sense of calmness, and a unifying material or plant will help to achieve this."

RIGHT An enigmatic piece of wood on a pedestal and the fuzz of grass *Miscanthus sinensis* 'Gracillimus' lie at the centre of the clean modernist lines in this Dutch garden.
DESIGN BY LUC ENGELHARD

Filling the space effectively

We have talked about gardens that 'borrow' trees and other aspects of the landscape from the surroundings, but what if your plot is adjacent to buildings and structures that you do not want to see and would rather shut out? Screening is sometimes possible, but often not. In this situation, the best solution is to focus the attention inwards. Conventional gardens have a tendency to do this, with planting around the outer edge of a lawn, but there are other, more interesting ways of directing the focus within the space.

Encouraging the eye to stay within the bounds of the garden and not stray beyond requires something to look at. There are two approaches here: one based on 'space', the other on its opposite, 'mass'. The 'space' solution is often seen in gardens where a sculpture or some other object of artistic interest is placed in the central area. Another, more subtle alternative, is to design a pattern of circular paving or other ground treatment that pulls the eye inwards. A pool or water feature is another option, and a very good one, since water has a powerful attraction for people. Garden-makers are often too cautious and limit the size, but a large pool in a small garden can be a good way of making a dramatic and relatively low-maintenance focal point. Planting can also play a role in drawing attention inwards. Using contemporary, almost meadow-style planting, intermingled with lower-level grasses and perennials, provides a visual richness of colour and texture and offers a continual delight, alongside the range of insects and birds it attracts.

Mass appeal

More radically, the centre of the garden can be filled with 'mass' instead of 'space'. Many gardeners want to fill their gardens with plants, which, for the plant collector is a viable and often desirable solution. The question is, and it is a very personal one, how many plants should you include and how big should they be? One idea is to fill the garden with perennials and shrubs and design a path between them – the experience will be one of penetrating a jungle where there is no distant or medium-range view. This idea may only appeal to a minority and goes against the instincts of many designers. But for those who love plants, it is an exciting proposition and by packing in as much experience as possible into a small space, it represents one of the most effective design tricks of all.

A similar but less overwhelming idea is to use planting that is under shoulder height, which provides plenty for visitors to see but reduces the feeling of claustrophobia. A great advantage of planting a small garden so fully is that it makes the experience truly immersive: once inside, you're in a world of your own.

LEFT This wide but shallow Dutch garden has been designed with a complex, abstract pattern at ground level to engage the eye and pull the focus into the centre.
DESIGN BY CAROLIEN BARKMAN

"A great advantage of planting a small garden so fully is that it makes the experience truly immersive."

LEFT Medium-sized to large grasses and small trees form an ambitious and confident planting scheme in this small space. In summer its lushness and complexity will keep the attention from wandering over the boundaries, while in winter seed heads provide interest.
DESIGN BY KWEKERIJ VAN NATURE

Interesting the feet

Just as the eyes should be kept busy, entertained, and stimulated, so should the feet. Designers of traditional Japanese gardens deliberately changed path surfaces every now and again in order to alter the walking experience. Doing this too often militates against the 'less is more' philosophy, but it is worth bearing in mind as a technique to keep our bodies interested as we negotiate the garden.

Other techniques that slow the pace and make us pay attention include breaking up paths and routes. The perpendicular perspective of Western classical design is again unhelpful in this respect – straight paths show us exactly where we are going, and take us directly there – boring! Breaking a path so that it suddenly changes direction delays the journey time, making us look in a different direction, and in doing so, see and experience different things. A straight path can be broken in two and given a kink part of the way down. Even more effective is the Chinese idea of the staggered path, one that reaches its destination by forcing the walker to change direction several times.

Stepping up

Many designers include different levels to heighten the drama in small spaces. Steep, narrow steps convey a sense of speed, while wide, low steps slow the pace. Even if a change in level is not strictly speaking necessary, a step has the same effect as a change in direction – it slows us down and enriches our experience. Just a 10cm (4in) drop from one area of the garden to the next will produce a similar effect to subdividing it.

If there are no changes in level for foot traffic, you can use raised beds to increase the visual interest and add subtly to the perception that the space is larger than it really is. Raising a bed requires constructing some sort of retaining wall, however low, which in itself can become a feature of interest or double as a seat. In larger retaining walls, you can also include holes for plants to poke out.

When considering where to site your raised beds, remember that they look most natural where they seem to be necessary, which basically means that they should back onto a bank or vertical structure that makes them appear as if they have a role to play.

TOP LEFT Changes in level slow the pace and can make a garden seem larger. The fern, *Matteuccia*, edging the path, also creates a sense of enclosure. DESIGN BY HOF TER DIEREN

CENTRE LEFT Decking offers a flexible way to make changes of level, while foliage planting enhances a narrow border. DESIGN BY ROBERT BROEKEMA

BOTTOM LEFT Even shallow raised beds will increase the visual interest in a small garden, while colourful planting, such as *Sedum* 'Herbstfreude', lavender, and white *Calamintha nepeta* fill space well and encourage the visitor to look down. DESIGN BY IN GOEDE AARDE

Injecting detail

A unified look is important for the whole garden but, at a more intimate level, detail and interest are also required. Detail helps to slow down the garden experience – the more there is to look at, the longer the garden journey becomes – and it can be introduced with plants, sculptural touches, and materials.

For most small gardens, the bulk of the detail will be in the planting. The colour green is a great unifier (which does *not* necessarily apply to variegated, bronze or golden foliage), and provides a neutral backdrop for detail in the form of other plants with different habits, such as leaf shape, size, and texture.

Narrow paths through planting slow progress further, almost forcing the visitor walking along them to take notice of what is on either side and to stop and look at attractive plant combinations. Too narrow, of course, and access along the path will be difficult, especially after rain pulls down the plant growth and soaks you.

Small surprises, such as sculptural 'found' objects or even rusted and disused tools, offer a good way to halt progress and make people stop and look. Place them strategically to surprise or intrigue your visitors. Fine detail on materials or structures also demands closer inspection – particularly useful are patterns or inscriptions that cannot be read from far away, and so do not break the visual unity of the whole space, but will be noticed at close range.

ABOVE There is detail in profusion in this plant-lover's garden, while the narrow pathway slows the pace and makes us look at what's on offer. Containers ensure there is always something of interest on display and offer flexibility, since they are easily swapped when the main performance is over.
DESIGN BY HERMIONE FRANKEL

FAR LEFT Placing decorative items on steps is one way of increasing detail, making the journey eventful and helping the mind to focus on the here and now.
DESIGN BY ZAKI & RUTH ELIA

LEFT This pile of stones held together by a motal rod makes a simple but effective piece of rustic artwork, which can be used to inject interest into dark corners of the garden.
DESIGN BY ELSA DAY

Introducing focal points and perspective

Tricks with perspectives tend to emphasise the length of the garden, and one of the easiest ways to do this is to use lines that run along its axis. Decking, for example, should be laid longitudinally, at 90 degrees to the house or main viewing point. Rectangular paving slabs likewise; reducing the gaps between the shorter sides of rectangular pavers, so that those closer to the house are larger than those at a distance, will also make a path or patio look longer.

When looking ahead we subconsciously scan for clues about distances. Our minds are easily fooled, and for centuries architects and designers have manipulated spaces to make us think that a garden or landscape is larger or more magnificent than it really is. A popular device is to use seemingly parallel lines to confuse the mind's sense of perspective. We are used to seeing features bound by paths, paving or canal-shaped ponds, and we know that the lines will converge as we look into the distance. But if, instead of being parallel, the lines are brought closer together towards the end of the garden, our minds over-calculate the distance and it looks longer.

Sharpening the focus

The use of perspective is related to the placement of focal points. A focal point is an eye-catcher, it seizes our attention and makes us look straight at it. As we have just seen, in a small garden, focal points can be used to manipulate our perception of distance, but we have also learned that looking straight ahead or having your attention grabbed by an object or plant is not always effective in restricted spaces. In these gardens, visitors need to be rewarded for looking around, paying attention to detail, and being diverted

Focal points need to be subtle in a small space or they will end up dominating the design. They should distil the experience of the whole and offer a counterpoint to more widely distributed features. An example could be a plant with large ornate foliage set among a mass of others with smaller and less distinguished leaves. Another option would be a focal point, such as a sculpture or tree, in the centre of the garden that leads the eye to the internal space rather than the boundaries.

When considering focal points, be aware that some can be unintentional. Any large, bright, dramatic or unexpected feature or plant may draw the eye, which is a problem if it is not part of the plan. Large or glossy leaves leap forward, as do the colours yellow, orange, and bright pink, while small leaves and the colour blue visually recede into the distance. The wise gardener places bold foliage, dramatic structures and attention-seeking colours near the house, or along the main viewing point.

LEFT The lower limbs of the purple plum, *Prunus cerasifera* 'Pissardii', are trimmed to shape it into a dramatic focal point.
DESIGN BY ANNIE GUILFOYLE

ABOVE TOP The grass *Hakonechloa macra* firmly but softly frames the end point of a pathway, marked by a simple wooden seat.
DESIGN BY LEEN GOEDEGEBUURE

ABOVE Water always adds a point of focus to a garden, the mind locking onto its mesmerising movement and sound.
DESIGN BY PAUL COX

Taking the gaze up

We have already noted the importance of vertical surfaces, which in many small gardens will be the boundaries. They are not only a surface to be used as part of the design, or perhaps hidden if unattractive, but can also add to the sense of space. Anything that raises the eyes upwards takes attention away from a limited ground space, as well as lifting the gaze towards the sky and light. A tall element literally takes your design upwards, extending and making more of the garden. It can also express a kind of confidence, suggesting that this is your space and your bit of sky to do with whatever you like.

While verticals offer the maximum impact for the minimum use of ground space, repeating a narrow vertical feature will also develop a strong sense of rhythm. Some of the most effective planting designs include repeated slim, vertical plants, such as upright box topiary, set out regularly and formally, or in a random pattern. Other elements, such as coloured poles, can be used likewise. They lend character and, crucially, provide visual unity, allowing the inclusion of more disparate features while still working as one.

BELOW LEFT *Clerodendrum trichotomum* is a good tree for a sunny, sheltered garden, and raises up the focus when the scented flowers appear in summer and again in autumn when the berries form.
DESIGN BY GARDENS OF APPELTERN

BELOW RIGHT In this small garden dominated by cool foliage, simple coloured columns provide year-round interest and a vertical element that directs the eye up to the sky.
DESIGN BY MENEER VERMEER

Combining functional spaces

The key to packing as much as possible into a small garden is making a single space fulfil more than one function. Designer Annie Guilfoyle suggests using the space beneath a seat or bench as storage for toys or other garden paraphernalia. Indeed, any kind of box-like structure can double as seating and storage, especially if it has cupboard-style doors and a flat, or nearly flat, top.

A bike box or storage space can also become part of the garden design and include a green roof of succulent sedum species or, with a little more soil depth, some herbs or rockery-type plants. With slightly deeper soil, you will have space for salad crops, but check that the construction of the box can take the weight first.

Stacking up

When choosing garden equipment or furniture, look for items that stack or fold up. A folding table and chairs allow for occasional outdoor meals, but can be put away to leave space for sunbathing and games, or just a sense of space, for the rest of the time.

Garden views, especially in urban plots, can be cluttered with unwanted but vital, functional objects, such as drainage pipes, air conditioning units, ducting and, on the ground, inspection covers. Vertical pipes can sometimes be boxed in, although if they ever need attention, this may present a problem. Screening is often a better option, especially if the structure includes panels that can be easily removed. Screens made from trellis can also support climbing plants and blend well into a garden setting, but they are more difficult to remove, unless you choose a species that will grow back rapidly after being cut down, such as ivy.

Inspection covers are often problematic, as they must be accessible but are frequently situated where they are difficult to hide with paving or decking. A good solution is to put a container of plants on top, although if the location is not an obvious place for a pot it may actually have the opposite effect and draw attention to the cover underneath. Any container used for this purpose also needs to be light enough to move relatively easily.

> "A bike box or storage space can become part of the garden design and could also include a green roof of succulent sedums."

TOP RIGHT A small shed with a green roof becomes an integral part of the garden design, while wooden objects form an unusual sculpture installation. DESIGN BY ANNIE GUILFOYLE & JAMES STEWART

BOTTOM RIGHT The green roof on this shed echoes the colours of plants in the garden. On very shallow green roofs, sedums, which come in a range of foliage colours, are the best choice. DESIGN BY TERESA DAVIES, STEVE PUTNAM & SAMANTHA HAWKINS

Including sensory experiences

Garden design, like so much of our design culture, is focused on sight. And while gardens for the partially-sighted prompt designers to think about our other senses, surely we should all be able to appreciate touch, scent, and even sound in the garden. Taste, of course, is enjoyed by fruit, vegetable, and herb growers.

Scent is evanescent but the small garden owner has an advantage, since fragrance is far more likely to be trapped within its confines. A warm wall provides the perfect place for tazetta daffodils in spring, honeysuckle in summer, phlox in autumn, and jasmine in winter, each releasing their sensual molecules, which give our hearts such a lift. Plant scents vary between those you need to plunge your nose into, like roses, those that carry a long way, such as the jasmines, and fragrant foliage, which often has to be brushed to release its fragrance.

BELOW LEFT *Trachelospermum jasminoides* is a first-rate climber for sheltered gardens, and features evergreen foliage and sweetly scented tiny white summer flowers.

BELOW CENTRE *Phormium* 'Jester' is a very popular plant for a centrepiece or focal point. Its linear leaves have a smooth, glossy texture, offering tactile and visual appeal.

BELOW RIGHT There are varieties of water lily (*Nymphaea* species) that do not need deep water to thrive, making them a very flexible option for the small garden. Water lilies benefit from a minimum of water disturbance, so don't be tempted to plant them close to a fountain or waterfall.
DESIGN BY SPENCER VINER

Sensitive to the touch

Touching plants may not only release their scent, but also allows us to appreciate their tactile qualities. Everyone should close their eyes and feel plants now and again: their textures, leaf sizes and shapes, stems, buds, even their spines and thorns. Such contact offers an opportunity to learn more about your plants.

Finally, there is sound. Classical Chinese gardeners considered the soundscape of the garden an important feature: the sound made by rain on leaves or the buzz of bees, for example, which enhance the visitor's experience. Opportunities for attractive sound in the garden are limited but not negligible – think of the rustling of grasses or bamboos in the wind.

Most garden makers who add sound to a garden do so with water, and features that offer a recognisable tinkling or splashing can effectively drown out or disguise urban noise. The best features are convincing – water spouts, for example, are more likely to be interpreted as 'real' than free-standing gushing pots. Sculptural water features like the latter draw attention and are best treated as focal points.

Linking the house and garden

Small gardens offer more opportunities to make a direct link between house and garden than larger properties. The closeness of the garden and limited expanse of terracing inevitably unites them more intimately. French windows or bifold patio doors also mean that the garden is only a few steps away, and by carefully framing a view of the outdoor space, you can shut out the boundaries, neighbours and town or city, and focus on the lush greenery, convincing the onlooker that they are somewhere else entirely. A focal point, just glimpsed at the end of a vista, can be particularly effective when viewed from inside.

Making connections

Some people choose a planting scheme to reflect the colours of the rooms that overlook the garden. While this is a little precious and perhaps unrealistic, unity can be created with common or repeated elements: ceramic containers, sculptural features, and paving of a similar size and colour inside and out.

Since many people like to eat outside, the proximity of the kitchen to the garden is an important factor to consider when planning an extension or refurbishment. This also works the other way round, as some cooking activities, such as barbecuing or baking in a clay oven, can only be performed outside, and there may be situations where the food needs to be prepared in the garden and eaten inside.

LEFT Generous floor-to-ceiling bifold doors offer the perfect way to integrate the house and garden. The house floor here is a little higher than the garden, affording a good vantage point. DESIGN BY JOANNE BERNSTEIN

CASE STUDY: Design tricks

Design by Annie Guilfoyle

This long and skinny garden initially resembled a bowling alley, according to designer Annie Guilfoyle. Although it is a private garden, the owners, James Stewart and Johnny Zimmer, also use it as a gallery space for small-scale sculpture exhibitions, as well as for entertaining. Annie's design links the house and garden by reflecting the brick and flint walls of the property with a paved terrace made from reclaimed granite setts. The three-storey house has a gallery on the first floor, which means the design has to look good from above, and displaying sculpture requires separate spaces, each with their own character. Annie has fulfilled the brief by dividing the garden into distinct areas, and these intimate rooms also create a successful social garden, ideal for parties.

DESIGN TRICKS USED

1. Glass balcony, offering an overview of the garden, but much is enticingly concealed

2. Terrace, from which only hints of the garden are seen

3. Planting, with space for sculptures

4. Steps enhance the space

5. Granite sett circle set into gravel pulls focus inwards

6. Planting backed by tiered hedges

7. Water feature, acts as a focal point (not seen)

8. Second paved seating area, invisible from the terrace by the house

9. Decking, partially screened by hedges

GARDEN DIMENSIONS:
Approx 22m x 9m (72ft x 30ft)

CLOCKWISE FROM TOP LEFT:

VIEW TO THE HOUSE
The use of reclaimed granite setts for the terrace adjacent to the property links the period house with the garden, creating a unified design.

PLANTING IN LAYERS
Foliage rules here – there are few flowers – which keeps the garden feeling trim and fresh throughout the year. Evergreens, including bay and loquat, offer winter interest, while the graphic layering of plants of different heights also adds contrasting foliage shapes, textures, and colours.

CREATING A JOURNEY
The gaps in the hedges, which allow passage from one part of the garden to another, are off-centre, preventing too much being seen at once. Walking those extra few metres from one part to another also helps to create the impression that this is a larger space.

JUST AN ILLUSION
The geometry of the paving and of the garden spaces creates a strong sense of structure. Such classical design is more typical of larger gardens, but on this scale, it helps sustain the illusion of the garden being larger than it really is.

HEDGING BETS
Hedging in this garden plays an important role, subdividing the space into three distinct areas. A 'stilt hedge' of pleached limes screens the central area, allowing glimpses through, but not all the way to the end of the garden.

3

Layering with plants

Nature's way

Exploring the ways in which plants grow together in communities in the wild provides us with a model of how they can be combined in a small garden, providing year-round interest in the tiniest of spaces.

Walk on the wild side

While some gardens are constructed without plants, the absence of green living things in a space dubbed a 'garden' is more often than not a gimmick. For most people, a garden is inconceivable without plants, either to admire or to eat – or both. Selecting the right combination of plants for your site can be one of the most difficult aspects of garden design, but with a little knowledge, you can create successful planting schemes that provide year-round colour and interest.

We will consider how to choose specific plants for your garden in Chapter 4, but first we need to look at them more holistically, as 'vegetation'. Rarely growing in isolation, plants form complex communities that fit together in distinct layers, which may be interpreted spatially (in other words, visually) or temporally through time. By learning how to combine them in this way, you will be able make the most of your small space. This may mean squeezing a huge amount of plant diversity into your small garden, or choosing a more limited number of species that work well together, which will make a cleaner and more graphic impact and require the minimum of maintenance.

One of the best ways of appreciating how plants organise themselves into layers is to take a walk in a natural or semi-natural environment. A forest is a good place to start. Here, you will see how the trees form an upper canopy, much of which is of a similar height. On the forest floor, there is usually another layer of plants, which by necessity are shade-tolerant. Below this is yet another layer, comprising very small plants, such as mosses. You may also notice an additional layer: an understorey, made up of shrubs or small trees that grow beneath the taller tree canopy.

Lighter edging

At the very edge of the woodland, a much more complex layering can be seen. Here, in the lighter conditions where sun is able to filter through the foliage, shrubs tend to dominate what is known as the 'woodland edge' habitat. This environment often includes a rich diversity of climbing plants and perennials, too, with small plants flourishing beneath larger ones, and even smaller types below those. It is worth spending time looking at how all these plants mesh together, since woodland edge habitats provide a good analogy for the borders in your garden, where a large number of species survive in close proximity.

In natural environments, plants organise themselves into layers on ecological principles, with shade plants beneath sun-lovers, but in the garden, it is also useful to think about 'visual layering'. This is when plants are combined to create an attractive composition, rather than the often confusing picture that nature offers.

LEFT This garden illustrates some of the planting layers that also make up natural communities: trees, climbers and ground-level perennials. Shrubs are missing but may take up too much space here.
DESIGN BY MAAYKE DE RIDDER

ABOVE Perennial planting has been combined to create a visual layering of plant colour and form, with *Aster* x *frikartii* 'Mönch' taking centre stage and *Calamagrostis brachytricha* at the rear. Geraniums and *Alchemilla mollis* make up the layer at ground level.
DESIGN BY LUMINE SWAGERMAN

PREVIOUS PAGE Hedging and flowering shrubs, *Clerodendrum* and *Hydrangea*, create the upper and middle layers in this town garden.
DESIGN BY GARDENS OF APPELTERN

Structural plants

Before going on any further, we need to look at the growth forms of plants, such as trees, shrubs, climbers, and perennials, which create the building blocks of both natural plant communities and those in gardens.

Each plant form behaves differently over time. Trees and shrubs accumulate growth year on year; herbaceous plants, such as perennials and bulbs, die back every year, disappearing below ground at the end of the growing season; annuals die at the end of the season, leaving their seed to produce the next generation of plants.

Getting to grips with trees

Visually the most imposing plants on the planet, trees in small gardens can be a blessing or a curse – sometimes both. Their shade in sunny plots may be welcome in the heat of summer, but in other areas they may cast a depressing pall and restrict plant choices. And while a flowering tree is a magnificent sight when in full bloom, its shade can be a burden for the rest of the year when it is in leaf.

Although many of us have to live with trees that others have planted, we need to view them in a positive light and make the most of the environments they create. We also need to plant trees ourselves that will perform effectively in our small spaces.

Trees have three main ecological impacts on their immediate environment, which you need to consider.

- They cast shade, which may be year long, as is the case with evergreens and conifers, restricting growth beneath them. Or, if the trees are deciduous, the shade will be temporary, allowing some plants to survive beneath the canopies.
- They extract moisture from the soil during the growing season, drying out the surrounding area.
- They extract nutrients from the soil, making it more difficult to grow plants beneath them.

To survive, plants need three main elements – light, water, and nutrients – all of which are restricted by trees. If levels of soil moisture and nutrients are high, but light is limited, a wide range of plants, including

"**Visually the most imposing plants on the planet, trees in small gardens can be a blessing or a curse – sometimes both.**"

many thought of as sun-lovers, may thrive well enough. In lightly shaded areas where moisture and nutrient levels are low, plant choices are restricted to shade-tolerant plants that grow naturally in woodlands, often referred to as 'woodland species'. Dry shade, where light, water and nutrients are all restricted, is the worst scenario, and only a few tough evergreens, such as English ivy (Hedera helix) and holly (Ilex), will grow well in these conditions. An ideal environment for the small garden is a shady area with moist (not waterlogged), reasonably fertile soil, which will allow you to grow a range of plants, including ferns and some wonderful woodland species. Your choice of tree will facilitate these ideal conditions.

Trees can be divided into two ecological categories: the long-lived trees of mature forests and short-lived pioneer species. The latter are those that grow rapidly in open spaces – hence the term 'pioneer'. Pioneers are usually smaller and cast lighter shade, making them suitable for smaller gardens, but choose carefully as some, such as birches (Betula), have dense surface rooting systems that dry out the soil and restrict growth beneath them, while others, including cherries (Prunus) and crab apples (Malus), are deeply rooted, allowing more plants to thrive under their canopies. Mature forest trees tend to create problems for garden owners, as they cast dense shade and their roots suck moisture from the soil. In addition, their annual deposit of leaf litter can affect the local environment, and ranges from heavy, slow-to-decay leaves, typical of maples (Acer species), to the lighter, quick-to-decay, nutrient-rich leaves of oaks (Quercus species). All can be good choices for the small garden, and the dense shade some create can be ameliorated by removing the lower branches to develop a 'high canopy', allowing in more sun, as well as direct light in the mornings and evenings when the sun comes in at a sharper angle.

Most woodland trees grow cheek by jowl, but there is considerable variation in their size and habit. The understorey layer that forms beneath the highest canopy is made up of shade-tolerant trees and shrubs, including evergreens, such as camellias and hollies, that survive by trapping the sun's energy year-round. Others are deciduous, and include some cherries, Asian maples (Acer), and dogwoods (Cornus), which benefit from the shade and shelter the taller trees afford.

LEFT Japanese maples, such as *Acer palmatum* 'Osakazuki', are a boon for small gardens as they stay small and have a distinctive branching habit. Immediately below this acer is the conifer *Thujopsis dolabrata*.
DESIGN BY GARDENS OF APPELTERN

RIGHT An *Aralia elata* makes a dramatic silhouette against the skyline in this rooftop garden. One of the most distinctive trees for small spaces, its upright habit allows other plants to flourish below.
DESIGN BY KWEKERIJ VAN NATURE

FAR RIGHT *Malus* x *robusta* 'Red Sentinel', an ornamental crab apple, has large white flowers that emerge from pink buds in spring. Its inedible raw fruit can, however, be used to make colourful jam.
DESIGN BY GARDENS OF APPELTERN

Shrubs for small spaces

Most shrubs are smaller than trees and rather than growing from a single trunk they have a multi-stemmed habit. However, the distinction between trees and shrubs is a hazy one, as some species are capable of being shrubs in some situations and small trees in others. Shrubs are very useful to gardeners for many reasons:

- They provide visual mass, helping to break up and subdivide the space.
- Many have attractive flowers, usually in spring, sometimes followed by colourful berries.
- Some have ornamental foliage and stems, and include varieties grown for their leaf colour and shape, or branching habit.
- They contribute greatly to biodiversity: birds use them for food, roosting and nesting.

Many shrubs grow too big for small gardens, and it is easy to plant them too densely – one trip to the garden centre may result in several days of hard work ten years later. Older gardens, in particular, often reflect the legacy of shrubs' popularity (and the relative unpopularity of perennials) in the late 20th century and may include overgrown specimens. When planting new shrubs in your small garden, take care not to make the same mistake and note their eventual sizes at the outset to ensure they are suitable.

An overwhelming majority of shrubs also have a shape most politely described as 'ambiguous', and will spread out in many directions over time, but the fact that they are also extremely resilient means that they can be kept smaller. Most are continually regenerating from the base and can be hacked back to rejuvenate them or maintain their size. The lower branches can also be cut away to create a planting space below the canopy and to make a feature of the stems, which would normally be hidden. The creation of these 'understorey' planting spaces is particularly useful for short, spring-flowering perennials and bulbs, species that in many cases would naturally grow beneath shrubs in the wild.

TOP LEFT *Pittosporum tenuifolium* 'Irene Paterson' is a slow-growing form with attractive dense evergreen foliage that makes a good year-round feature in gardens with mild winter climates.

CENTRE LEFT *Rhododendron* 'Victorine Hefting' is a compact Japanese azalea with a layered branching habit. All azaleas flower in late spring and can be clipped to shape.

BOTTOM LEFT The hardy *Fuchsia magellanica* forms a sizeable bush in mild-winter areas, where it is valued for its profuse summer flowers or used as a decorative hedging plant.

RIGHT The layers in this scheme include clipped box creating the middle layer and leafy perennials providing texture and shape at ankle height.
DESIGN BY JACQUELINE VAN DER KLOET

MASTERCLASS
SCULPTING WITH WOODY PLANTS

Trees and shrubs are known as 'woody plants' and they have relatively plastic growth, which allows them to be shaped and sculpted. This is a huge boon to owners of small gardens, and means species that would normally grow huge can be kept much smaller. Woody plants can also be shaped in a creative way to produce graphic images and distinctive shapes that contrast with the softer, less visually defined forms of perennials and annuals.

Woody plants vary enormously in how they react to being cut. Some species, such as pines and birches, react badly and cannot be shaped, while the majority respond moderately well to cutting, and a few, including box (*Buxus sempervirens*), respond so well, it is more common to see them clipped than not.

We can also divide the 'good responders' into two main groups:

- Species that only throw out straight new stems when cut; e.g. willows (*Salix* species) and hazels (*Corylus* species).
- Species that can be cut repeatedly and send out dense, twiggy growth; e.g. box (*Buxus sempervirens*), yew (*Taxus baccata*), and beech (*Fagus sylvatica*).

These plants' positive response to cutting has led to many different uses for them. In the small garden, we can employ the following techniques to fit them most effectively into our limited space.

Pollarding and coppicing

Pollarding is where a tree trunk is cut at about head height, from which point it sends out masses of new straight shoots. Trees, such as willows, are often cut in this way every year, and the resulting new shoots are traditionally used for basket-making. In the garden, pollards can be used for screening, with the new growth providing coverage for at least half the year. The winter colour of young willow bark is also very attractive, and often the brightest feature in the garden at that time.

Coppicing describes the pruning technique where a large shrub or tree is cut regularly to ground level. The rod-like stems that emerge can be used for fencing and building and were once a vital part of the rural economy. Coppicing is also useful to the modern gardener, allowing you to limit tree species to the dimensions of a medium-sized shrub. The leaf size of most trees the year after coppicing is also twice as large as normal. *Paulownia tomentosa*, in particular, grows enormous leaves when cut annually.

Pleaching

This is another historical technique, used for making a hedge-like screen above head height. Very popular in the Netherlands and Belgium, it takes skill to start from scratch, but pre-pleached trees are available from specialist nurseries. Pleaching is traditionally used for limes (*Tilia* species) but the following also respond well: *Carpinus betulus*, *Gleditsia triacanthos*, *Malus* species, *Photinia*, *Platanus*, and *Quercus ilex*.

OPPOSITE Columns of hornbeam add structure to a garden otherwise dominated by grasses and perennials. They should be clipped twice a year.
DESIGN BY LEEN GOEDEGEBUURE

ABOVE LEFT A *Catalpa bignonioides*, pollarded to form a lollipop, will over the summer grow larger and looser in habit. Prune annually to achieve the effect.
DESIGN BY GARDENS OF APPELTERN

ABOVE RIGHT Pleached lime trees create a 'partial hedge', offering screening for privacy at a crucial level but allowing access and sightlines below. Once established, maintaining a pleached hedge is straightforward.
DESIGN BY ERVE ODINCK

Cornus alba 'Sibirica'

TREES AND SHRUBS FOR COPPICING

- *Acer pensylvanicum*
- *Carya* species (warm summer climates only)
- *Catalpa* species
- *Cercis* species (for foliage only, as coppicing will prevent flowering)
- *Cornus alba, C. sanguinea, C. stolonifera* (for coloured winter stems)
- *Corylus* species (hazel)
- *Cotinus coggygria* (smoke bush)
- *Eucalyptus* species
- *Liriodendron tulipifera* (tulip tree)
- *Paulownia* species
- *Pterocarya* species
- *Quercus* species (oak)
- *Salix alba* (for coloured winter stems)
- *Salix fargesii* and *S. magnifica* (for foliage)
- *Sambucus* species (elder)
- *Tilia* species (lime)

HEDGING TREES AND SHRUBS FOR SMALL GARDENS

- *Berberis thunbergii* varieties (pictured)
- *Buxus sempervirens* (box)
- *Carpinus betulus* (hornbeam)
- *Cotoneaster franchetii* and many other small-leaved *Cotoneaster* species
- *Euonymus fortunei* varieties
- *Ilex crenata* (Japanese holly)
- *Lonicera nitida* (shrubby honeysuckle)
- *Osmanthus x burkwoodii*
- *Pittosporum tenuifolium* 'Variegatum'
- *Prunus lusitanica* (Portuguese laurel)
- *Rhododendron* (small-leaved evergreen Japanese azalea types)
- *Taxus baccata* (yew)
- Bamboo – common hedging material in Japan, but as we shall see, many types have running roots; the shoots need frequent cutting too. It may frighten the neighbours.

Berberis thunbergii f *atropurpurea* (left) and
B. thunbergii f *atropurpurea* 'Harlequin' (right)

Hedging

Among the oldest and most commonly used pruned features of all, hedges fall broadly into two categories: the farm hedge and the garden hedge. The former, which tends to take up a lot of sideways space, only has a place in gardens that are trying to be self-consciously rustic or are prioritising wildlife. Garden hedges are kept neatly trimmed, generally up to a maximum width of 60cm (2ft), but remember that their hungry roots will spread out further on either side. Although a wall or fence, or a trellis with climbing plants, may be a more sensible option where space is tight, if it fits, a hedge makes an attractive backdrop for planting and forms part of the visual layering of the garden.

When choosing a hedging species, research them thoroughly and bear in mind the following factors:

- **Rate of growth** Too slow and you will lose patience; too fast and you will be cutting it several times a year and worrying your neighbours.
- **Eventual size** This has some relationship to rate of growth, as very vigorous species generally end up large. Do not expect a species that rapidly reaches a desired height to then stay that size; in reality, it will continue to grow quickly. A hedge will have to be cut at least once a year to maintain the same size. Also check that your chosen species will not be too short for your needs.
- **Evergreen or deciduous** Decide whether you want leaves all year, or choose a deciduous species that changes with the seasons. There is also a middle path here, as beech (*Fagus sylvatica*) and hornbeam (*Carpinus betulus*) retain their dead leaves through the winter.
- **Leaf colour** Variegated foliage can make a garden lighter, but it is not always the best backdrop for other plants as it can produce a confusing image. Dark foliage makes a good foil for other plants but can be depressing in small or shaded locations.

ABOVE LEFT Box (the paler shrub) can be clipped to maintain a small and tight shape, and has always been the favourite shrub for sculptural effects. Portuguese laurel is a larger plant with bigger leaves, which do not respond as well to tight clipping.

Topiary

Essentially, this is a hedging plant treated as sculpture. People tend to either love or hate topiary. Its advantage for small gardens is that it allows a large plant to fit into a restricted space and also creates a focal point to hold the gaze.

The rules are: keep shapes simple, do not get carried away, and remember that clipped shapes often look best when they produce a creative tension with soft, informal, even blowsy planting. Another suggestion is to forget the historical tendency towards the figurative, which always ends up looking like a squirrel, and keep to the abstract – contemporary topiary has a lot to offer. Not all woody plants traditionally used for topiary are suitable for small gardens; select those with smaller leaves and a dense branching habit which, with skilful clipping, can be cut to an almost knife-like edge.

Niwaki

Related to the art of bonsai (making of miniature trees), the Japanese technique known as niwaki is only just becoming familiar in the West. It creates miniature forests of trees, usually 3–5m (10–16ft) high, which thrive in extremely confined spaces.

RIGHT Clipping should be creative. Simplicity is often the best policy, such as with the box globes above, but new styles, including Japanese niwaki pruning (below right), offer exciting possibilities. Abstract expressionism does too, but it is practised by few.
DESIGN BY WILLY & JAN ALKEMA

PLANTS FOR TOPIARY

- *Buxus* species (pictured)
- *Carpinus betulus* (hornbeam)
- *Ilex crenata* (Japanese holly)
- *Lonicera nitida* (shrubby honeysuckle)
- *Phillyrea* species
- *Taxus baccata* (yew)

Compact sub-shrubs

Botanists fight shy of using the term sub-shrubs, but these small, woody plants are of enormous value to gardeners. Rarely more than a metre (39in) in height, they form compact hummocky shapes, have a dense, twiggy, branching habit, and very small leaves, which in some species are little more than needles or scales.

Sub-shrubs have many advantages for those with small gardens: they are compact, mostly evergreen, tolerate difficult conditions and need little maintenance. However, they are often short-lived (five to 20 years) and after around five to ten years they tend to deteriorate markedly. Most are from harsh environments: many are of Mediterranean origin (for example, lavender) or from high altitudes; others, such as heathers and hebes, are from moorlands.

Many sub-shrubs almost 'flow' around obstacles and into gaps. Their shapes are also pleasing, almost calming or cuddly, and it is tempting to use them for the bulk of the garden. The fact that many species have evergreen, grey or silver-tinged foliage adds to their appeal, and they are ideal for a planting style that counterposes clearly defined shapes.

Sub-shrubs are very useful for a visual graphic type of layering (see pp.62–63), but are not as suitable for naturalistic layering (see p.66). This is because they are nearly all sun-lovers, and react to a lack of light or overcrowding by losing their tidy shape or dying back. However, they perform the following invaluable roles in the small garden:

- Provide ground cover.
- Offer edging for paths and the front of borders.
- Fill horizontal space without taking up too much vertically.
- Contrast with other shapes, particularly ornamental grasses.
- Fill odd corners and round out rough edges.

If you live in an area where winters are not too cold and temperatures rarely dip below -20°C (4°F), you will have a good choice of sub-shrubs that suit your conditions. In mild-winter regions that experience only light frosts, your options will be wider and include a

broad range of Mediterranean species and the New Zealand hebes, which feature foliage in a wide range of colours, including the fresh greens rarely seen in other evergreen shrubs.

Reliable climbers

While relying on others for support, climbers are ideal for small gardens, taking up very little ground space. Their behaviour and habits are generally on a scale between two extremes:

- Lax shrubs with rather floppy growth, or arching species that can stand on their own but look better if supported or trained; e.g. some rose species.
- Obligate climbers, such as clematis, which in natural conditions do not survive unless they have something to climb up.

In nature, climbers tend to be most visible in woodland-edge habitats, where they drape themselves over shrubs and clamber up trees. Europe has few climbing species compared to North America or eastern Asia, but all are supremely useful for packing interest into a small space. Climbers offer colour and variety and they are the most important plants to consider when thinking about the vertical dimension in a small garden (see also Chapter 5, pp.108–119).

TOP FAR LEFT *Hebe albicans* forms a neat huddle beside a *Miscanthus* grass. Useful evergreen plants for milder areas, hebes have a tidy rounded shape and flower in summer, but, like all sub-shrubs, they do not live forever and will not respond well to pruning. DESIGN BY MERRIMENTS GARDENS

BOTTOM FAR LEFT Sub-shrubs, such as lavender and silvery *Artemisia pontica*, mix well with shorter grasses, such as this *Stipa calamagrostis*, which add a contrast in texture and form. DESIGN BY MERRIMENTS GARDENS

TOP LEFT The stems of climbing roses, such as 'Blushing Lucy' and 'Handel', shown here, need tying in to supports, but this extra care is worth it, as few other plants convey such summery romance. DESIGN BY JAN & ADDY TRAAS

LEFT *Parthenocissus quinquefolia* tends to put on its autumn colours very early, often in late summer, and retains its vibrant leaves for a number of months. It is one of the few self-clinging climbers and can easily reach up to the second storey of a house wall.

Herbaceous and short-lived plants

Perennial power

Also known as herbaceous perennials, these plants are now frequently the mainstay of smaller gardens. Most are compact, easy to grow and vigorous, and, unlike woody plants, they have the capacity to grow cheek by jowl alongside one another. During the winter, most die down, surviving underground as resting buds attached to root systems, which may be quite substantial. They will then reappear in spring. They also vary enormously in vigour, lifespan and their performance in the garden.

Perennials have a very distinct form, unique to each species, which is immutable – unlike many woody plants, it cannot be substantially altered by pruning or shaping. Understanding the forms of your chosen perennials and using them to your advantage is the key to working successfully with these plants. We grow most for their flowers and the colour they give us, but their structure is perhaps more important when creating a beautiful design. Many perennials also grow naturally under, or in close proximity to, other plants, so they are ideal for the smaller garden.

It is difficult to categorise perennials, and the following groupings present a pragmatic, evidence-based approach, designed to help you understand how best to layer and mesh them together.

> "Most perennial plants are compact, easy to grow and vigorous, and, unlike woody plants, they have the capacity to grow cheek by jowl alongside one another."

- **Long-lived clump-forming perennials** make up most of the range currently available. Plants form clumps that steadily increase in size, and do so predictably. Examples for the small garden include *Alchemilla mollis*, *Brunnera macrophylla*, *Geranium* species (pink plants above), *Nepeta* species (mauve plants above), and *Rudbeckia* species.

- **Long-lived static perennials** form clumps, but so slowly that this can be disregarded as a benefit. Many have deep or extensive root systems and are very long-lived. Examples include *Astilbe* species (above), *Eupatorium* species, *Euphorbia polychroma*, *Sedum spectabile*, and *Veronicastrum virginicum*.

- **Long-lived running perennials** send out underground runners and pop up between other plants, often 10–15cm (4–6in) away from the 'parent'. Most are not aggressive, but a few form a dominating mass of roots that cause neighbours to suffer. Examples include *Campanula poscharskyana* (above), *Euphorbia cyparissias*, and *Lysimachia punctata*.

- **Short-lived perennials** live for approximately three to ten years. They often have showy flowers and most have a long tap root and do not spread, except by seed, which is often freely produced. Examples include *Echinacea purpurea* (pink plants above), many *Achillea* and *Aquilegia* varieties, *Knautia macedonica*, and *Malva moschata*.

- **Evergreen perennials** are generally not evergreen but 'wintergreen', their leaves lasting through the winter to be replaced by fresh growth in spring. Their winter presence is useful in small gardens and most are long-lived clump-formers. Examples include many *Epimedium* species (above) and *Bergenia*, *Helleborus*, *Liriope*, and *Pulmonaria* species.

- **Ornamental grasses and grass-like plants** are grown for their flowers and seed heads, some for their foliage. Most are long-lived clump-formers; a few are noted runners and others can seed aggressively. Examples for the small garden include *Stipa tenuissima* (above), and species of *Carex*, *Molinia*, *Pennisetum*, *Sesleria*, and *Stipa*.

Annual interest

With a lifespan of just one year, these short-lived plants, together with biennials (see panel opposite), are the icing on the cake for many gardeners. They are genetically programmed to flower profusely, often for long periods, so that they have a high chance of producing seed to perpetuate the species. But annuals also have disadvantages. They need to be replaced every year, resulting in continual expenditure of time, effort and money. In addition, they offer little to look at early in the year before they have matured or later on after they have flowered.

Including short-lived plants in the garden is a very personal decision. Some people love them, and are prepared for the inevitable annual outlay, while others would rather opt for shrubs and long-lived perennials, relying on more permanent visual effects. Compromise is common, with many people choosing a shrub- and perennial-dominated garden, with spaces for annuals to provide a splash of summer colour. A popular solution is to grow annuals in containers which can then be dotted around the garden and moved out of the way when they are over.

Traditional garden practice has seen a lot of 'bedding out', where one group of plants is set out in spring, another in summer, with perhaps even a third replacement in autumn. Increasingly, this is seen as expensive, wasteful and unsustainable, but if you have the time, it is a useful way of maximising interest in a small space.

The different habits of the various annuals and biennials determine how they can be utilised to fit into the visual and naturalistic layers of the small garden (see pp.62–71). All of the following, except for the half-hardy plants, are likely to scatter their seed, so you may find some seedlings coming up each year. The results are unpredictable, but delightful.

> "A popular solution is to grow annuals in containers which can then be dotted around the garden."

- **Short-lived annuals** grow, flower, set seed, and die. Most annuals are sown in the spring, where they are to flower, which they tend to do spectacularly, if briefly. Sometimes it is possible to buy young plants in small containers (known as 'plugs') which can then be set out in the garden where you want them to perform. Examples include most poppies (*Papaver* species – above), cornflowers (*Centaurea cyanus*), *Limnanthes douglasii*, *Linum*, and *Schizanthus* varieties.

- **Half-hardy plants**, sold as bedding, may be annuals or perennials, but they do not survive frosts and will die in the winter. *Tagetes* marigolds are a classic example, along with varieties of *Cleome*, *Cosmos* (above), *Nemesia*, *Verbena*, and *Zinnia*.

- **Winter annuals** often last much longer than summer-flowering annuals. Many are from the Mediterranean, where the growing season starts in autumn and ends in summer. They are usually sown, or planted out, in spring, but if sown in autumn to grow slowly over winter, they will last much longer, especially where winters are mild and summers cool. Pansies are the classic example, but *Calendula* marigolds (above) and E*schscholzia* poppies will grow in winter to flower in the spring too.

- **Perennials grown as annuals** live for three years or more and tend to flower profusely for a long period, but as many are tender their survival is never guaranteed. Examples include *Pelargonium* (above), dahlias, petunias, begonias, and *Impatiens.*

INCLUDING BIENNIALS

These plants live for two years, as their name suggests. Biennials generally grow a rosette of leaves in the first year and then flower, set seed and die in the second. The rosette can take up a bit of space in a small garden, but the flowers are often carried on an economically narrow spike. Old cottage garden favourites, such as forget-me-nots, foxgloves (below top) and sweet Williams (below bottom) are biennials, and many self-seed around the garden, creating beautiful naturalistic effects. Other examples are wallflowers (*Erysimum* species), evening primrose (*Oenothera* species), *Eryngium giganteum*, *Verbascum* and, very often, hollyhocks (*Alcea* varieties) and lupins.

Bulb rewards

Plants that grow from bulbs are similar to annuals in that they are as near to 'instant' as you can expect in the plant world. They are, of course, chiefly associated with spring, but there are bulbs that flower in summer, such as lilies and gladioli, and in autumn, including colchicums (known incorrectly as 'autumn crocus') and the wild cyclamen C. *hederifolium*. Together with annuals, bulbs can be seen as the final decorative layer in the garden, another kind of icing on the cake.

Bulbs are ideal for new gardeners because they are so easy and rewarding. But while purchasing a few bulbs every year is fun, buying lots can be expensive, so how well will they flower again? To answer this question and determine their longevity, identify which of the following categories your chosen bulbs fall into.

LEFT The tulip 'Orange Emperor' dotted among early-flowering spurge (*Euphorbia cyparissias*) and brown-leaved sedge (*Carex comans*), is a good example of a harmonious colour scheme. Later-flowering perennials could be inserted to continue the interest.
DESIGN BY ARNAUD MAURIÈRES & ERIC OSSART

- **Potentially long-lived but vulnerable** Crocuses are good examples of bulbs that potentially flower again and spread, but are often eaten by mice or squirrels, or dug up by mistake when dormant. Many small bulbs suffer a similar fate, and in some cases they can also be a bit slow to form clumps. Other examples include: *Chionodoxa*, *Colchicum* (pictured) *Iris*, *Scilla*, *Ipheion*, and 'drumstick' alliums.

- **Long-lived, repeat flowering and almost indestructible** Daffodils (*Narcissus* – pictured) and snowdrops (*Galanthus*) are good examples of bulbs that not only flower again and again, if their leaves are not removed after flowering, but also increase every year, so a bulb soon becomes a small clump. Other examples include *Leucojum* and *Muscari*.

- **'Annual' bulbs** Tulips (pictured) are the main examples of annual bulbs. Hailing from Central Asia, with its hot dry summers, the tulips we buy are grown in a special way to ensure flowering, but once in the garden they cannot be guaranteed to bloom a second time. Some will, many will not, and they are best thought of as annuals.

The lawn

So far, the lawn has been the 'elephant in the room' – the all-important feature that has not been mentioned but which, for many, is such a crucial part of garden making. We have seen how rich and complex planting can be, even in a small space, and yet the lawn is quite the opposite, providing a simple, uniform carpet. The reason many gardens are dominated by a lawn is largely historical, and since much of the garden industry is related to lawn maintenance, there are massive vested interests in promoting turf when perhaps other ground treatments would be better. Let's look at the advantages and disadvantages for the small garden.

For

- Grass is green, refreshing, and good to look at.
- It makes a good foreground for planting, especially colourful border planting.
- Nothing beats grass to lie on, or as a children's play surface.
- A lawn, however small, reads 'real garden'; with hard surfaces there is always that nagging feeling that this is 'only a yard'.

Against

- Lawns need watering to look good year-round, which in some places is difficult and unsustainable.
- In small gardens they are likely to receive heavy foot traffic and when combined with less than ideal growing conditions, particularly shade, you may end up with mud rather than a lush grassy sward.
- Lawns need mowing, and if you have little space, where do you store the mower?

In the end, including a lawn is a personal decision, but bear in mind that it will be the single most time-consuming feature to maintain, even in a plant-filled garden.

LEFT A lawn as central space performs an important visual function, creating a strong, simple design, but it is too small for any real practical use.
DESIGN BY ERWIN STAM

TOP RIGHT Lawns can serve more than one function: here, the grass forms a series of gently-graded steps between cones of clipped yew, producing a dramatic design all year round.
DESIGN BY DE HEERENHOF

CENTRE RIGHT One of the most important uses of a lawn is as a play space for children. Lawns for family gardens need to be reasonably large to avoid play intruding into other areas.
DESIGN BY ROBERT BROEKEMA

BOTTOM RIGHT Lawn as sculpture? Gently domed ellipses of turf break up paving here, creating an unusual effect and absorbing water runoff.
DESIGN BY GARDENS OF APPELTERN

Visual plant layering

Three-layer principle

This design technique creates three layers of planting which produce a strong, graphic effect that is easy for us to interpret or 'read'. It works visually because we have a deep, probably hard-wired appreciation of things grouped into threes or divided into three.

Think back to the forest we discussed at the beginning of this chapter, and how it was often divided into tree canopy, shrub understorey and ground layer. This three-layer principle can be a useful basis for creating a simple planting scheme in the garden, and it is used by designers in Japan and elsewhere who have very limited spaces in which to work.

To combine your plants to produce these three layers, divide them into the following categories:

- **Upper Layer** Formed of plants at head height or taller.
- **Middle Layer** Made up of a bushy, visual mass.
- **Ground Layer** Plants that fill gaps below the middle layer, with space for annuals and bulbs.

The impact of this type of planting is dependent on some of the components being evergreen, and is most effective if it also includes a range of plant shapes that complement one another.

> "Creating a simple layering system results in a strong graphic effect that is easy for us to interpret or read."

Interest at ground level

In our natural example of a forest, we noticed that there was a very low-level ground-hugging layer. Beneath the small shrubs, ferns, wild flowers, or whatever else is growing at around knee-height, there is often a layer of plants that measure just a few centimetres. This may simply comprise moss, but sometimes includes flowering plants as well.

The ground-hugging layer is all too often forgotten by gardeners, but in a small space, every little counts. The more interest that can be packed in, the more the journey is slowed, and the better the overall effect. An advantage of creating a lot of interest at ground level is that it does not obstruct or complicate the big picture, but can be appreciated by those who care to take a closer look.

Very low-growing plants are commonly creeping perennials that root in as they spread. They tend to find ways through and between other plants or objects placed on the ground and if gaps in the paving are not filled with cement they will sometimes infiltrate in between the slabs too. A surprising profusion can be fitted in at such a low level. As we shall see later on, there is also a biodiversity advantage; covering the ground with a layer of vegetation allows a range of invertebrates to survive here, as it provides relative safety from predators. Examples of low-growing flowering plants range from the many forms of creeping thyme to the chunkier bergenias (see also p.71).

LEFT Climbers, such as this rose, are ideal for linking upper and lower layers in a garden, or for forming a middle layer of shrubs.
DESIGN BY JOKE VAN KOPPEN

RIGHT *Smyrnium perfoliatum* is a winter-growing annual that flowers in early summer and self-seeds if it likes the conditions in the garden. Here it forms a short-lived but spectacular middle layer between a clipped box, tulips and some clump-forming perennials.
DESIGN BY JACQUELINE VAN DER KLOET

MASTERCLASS
HOW TO LAYER WITH PLANTS

This small garden includes elements we find in the majority of gardens – trees, shrubs, perennials, and bulbs – but here they are carefully selected to lend a visual clarity to the plant combinations. Inevitably, there are compromises; for example, there are no unclipped shrubs or climbers, which results in a 'clean' composition, but limits the garden biodiversity.

The layers here lend the design structure and depth, while also ensuring there is plenty to hold the interest throughout the year. The upper layer includes an apple tree, a traditional choice, ideal for a small space. The middle layer is limited, and dominated by clipped box and a hedge, which together allow for clear sight lines across the garden. The restricted middle layer does have an advantage, which is to provide space for a full and complex ground-hugging layer.

THE UPPER LAYER

The Upper Layer here includes an apple tree.
You could also include:
- other small trees
- pollarded or pleached trees
- large shrubs, especially if the lower limbs are removed to allow underplanting
- a tall hedge
- climbers on a high wall
- trees or large shrubs in the next door garden, which are visually part of yours

Warning! The following may not work:
- fast-growing trees
- shrubs that take up too much sideways space
- large perennials or grasses, which usually have limited visual mass at height

THE MIDDLE LAYER

The Middle Layer here includes box topiary, grasses and tulips. You could include:
- medium-sized shrubs
- a hedge at no more than head height
- perennials or grasses with a long season of interest
- climbers on a wall or fence

Warning! The following might not work:
- shrubs that take up too much sideways space
- perennials or grasses with a limited season of interest
- upright perennials and grasses that have a tendency to flop over, especially in heavy rain

THE GROUND LAYER

The Ground Layer here includes low-growing geranium species, the shade-tolerant grass *Milium effusum* 'Aureum', and bluebells (foliage only).
You could include:
- low-growing shrubs or sub-shrubs
- perennials, grasses, ferns of appropriate height
- shorter annuals, biennials, and bulbs

Warning! The following might not work:
- ground-cover shrubs that make up in spread what they lack in height
- perennials that sprawl vigorously or untidily over paths or lawns
- perennials or annuals that grow upright rather than spreading

Naturalistic plant layering

Wild ecologies

Many of us love the 'wildness' of flower-rich natural or semi-natural habitats, but is it possible to transport some of this wildness to a small garden? It is, but you will find designing effective schemes easier with some understanding of how these plants fit together, spatially as well as seasonally. Creating wild looking, naturalistic planting on a small scale is very different to the more graphic type of visual layering we have discussed so far, where the layers are easy to identify.

Think of a natural or semi-natural grassland, like a hay meadow or a prairie. Unlike the forest we considered earlier, which has quite clearly visible and identifiable layers, this is a lot more confused. It might even look a bit of a mess, especially following the peak growing season. A traditional hay meadow, a stretch of prairie, or even an overgrown pasture can be surprisingly complex, and although they may be more difficult to see, there are layers here too, and appreciating what they comprise can help us to create more naturalistic planting schemes in our small gardens.

Cottage garden inspiration

Our starting point for this type of ecological layering is the 'cottage garden' tradition. This was essentially an early 20th century movement, initially largely British but eventually hugely influential all over the world.

The cottage garden was a romantic idealisation of the gardens of the rural poor, but it later ended up as a sophisticated way of creating seemingly undesigned, carefree plantings, where plants (mostly perennials) grow densely and apparently spontaneously. No bare ground is visible beneath the mass of plants, which, in many cases, are growing at a higher density than in more conventional schemes.

Recent developments in planting design apply a more naturalistic model when fitting plants together, based on an understanding of plant shape, referred to as their architecture, and rate of growth through the year. These are the main factors to consider when creating a cottage or naturalistic look in small gardens, and the following explanation of plant groups will help you to combine them most effectively.

ABOVE Lupins make a bold splash of colour at the front of a border, along with *Allium cristophii* and *Pennisetum alopecuroides*.

RIGHT Although ecological layering can create a rich and biodiverse garden, it may lack visual clarity, but by planting densely like this, you can pack in plenty of seasonal interest to add more colour and form.
DESIGN BY HERMIONE FRANKEL

COMBINING PERENNIAL PLANTS IN SMALL SPACES

When putting together layered planting combinations, it is useful to group perennials, bulbs and sub-shrubs in several overlapping categories, based on their shape and habit. This enables us to imagine how we might fit them together, filling space while not crowding them too much. These groups, and how to use the plants in them, are explained more fully overleaf.

① Small spring-flowering, summer-dormant bulbs and perennials

② Broad-leaved or wide-spreading foliage perennials

③ Clump-formers that produce leaf mass at low levels

④ Weak-stemmed plants

⑤ Narrow plants

⑥ Upright-growing perennials

⑦ Sub-shrubs

⑧ Ground-hugging plants

① Small spring-flowering, summer-dormant bulbs and perennials

These fit in almost anywhere because they come up early and die down early, so there is very little competition with plants that develop later. Most are between 15–30cm (6–12in) in height, and do not compete with later-flowering perennials for moisture and nutrients; they do not compete visually either. The exceptions are the larger daffodils, which have tall, often untidy looking foliage up to 40cm (16in) – these are best placed behind larger perennials so that the foliage can be hidden as it dies down.

SMALL SPRING FLOWERS & BULBS

- *Anemone blanda, A. nemorosa*
- *Chionodoxa* species
- *Corydalis* species
- *Crocus* species
- *Cyclamen coum* (pictured)
- *Galanthus* species
- *Mertensia* species
- *Narcissus* species (smaller types)
- *Primula* species – primrose and polyanthus types
- *Scilla* species
- *Viola* species

② Broad-leaved or wide-spreading foliage perennials

As we shall see later, these are very important for long seasons of interest in smaller gardens. They vary in how much and when they dominate the ground beneath them. Most form a leafy layer so close to the ground that they do not mix intimately with other plants, but this may not be relevant, since they need space to show off their leaves – they almost shout "don't cramp my style". Exceptions are the *Rodgersia* species, whose leaves emerge so late and on such long stems that early spring flowers and bulbs, like those listed left, can flourish beneath them.

SPREADING FOLIAGE PERENNIALS

- *Astilbe* – larger varieties
- *Epimedium* species
- Ferns
- *Helleborus* species
- *Heuchera* species
- *Hosta* species (pictured)
- *Phlomis russeliana*
- *Pulmonaria* species
- *Rodgersia* species
- *Saxifraga fortunei* varieties

③ Clump-forming perennials that produce leaf mass at low level

Many of these plants live naturally in high density environments and are used to being packed in tight. There is some overlap with weak-stemmed plants that need support (right). Geraniums are a good example and comprise a useful, colourful and versatile genus. While some, such as G. *sanguineum*, are quite short and tidy, a number, including G. *endressii*, are actually weak-stemmed.

CLUMP-FORMING PLANTS

- *Acanthus* species
- *Agapanthus* species
- *Alchemilla* species
- *Astrantia* species
- *Centaurea montana*
- *Echinacea* species
- *Euphorbia* species
- *Geranium* species
- *Geum* species
- *Hemerocallis* species (pictured)
- *Iris sibirica*
- *Kniphofia* species
- *Lupinus* species
- *Nepeta* species
- *Origanum* species
- *Papaver orientale*
- *Persicaria* species
- *Rudbeckia* species
- *Salvia* (European hardy species)
- *Sedum* (upright, late-flowering species)
- Grasses: *Stipa tenuissima, Deschampsia cespitosa, Pennisetum, Sporobolus heterolepis*

④ Weak-stemmed perennials

These are liable to drive tidy gardeners a bit crazy as they send out colourful flowers on long, thin, rangy stems. In nature, they grow in environments where their stems lean on other plants for support, particularly on grasses or stronger or more upright perennials. Some clump-forming species (left) have this tendency too. Planting them at high density so that their stems can sprawl out, up and over other plants is the only sensible way of growing them. There are also some, such as *Nepeta*, which seem to form tidy clumps without creating problems, but also work very well if allowed to run through other plants.

WEAK-STEMMED PLANTS

- *Calamintha* species
- *Centaurea* species
- *Euphorbia cyparissias, E. polychroma*
- *Geranium pratense*
- *Knautia macedonica*
- *Linaria* species
- *Nepeta* species
- *Potentilla* species
- *Sanguisorba* species (pictured)

⑤ Narrow perennials and bulbs

These are very often short-lived species that do not spread sideways but prioritise flowers and seed heads held on strong, self-supporting, upright stems. Consequently they do not elbow other plants aside and are ideal for small garden schemes. They have a strong tendency to self-sow and insinuate themselves among other plants, popping up here and there to create a carefree, spontaneous effect. Some, like *Geranium sylvaticum*, are not generally short-lived yet still often seed around, but take up so little space they do not compete with others.

NARROW PERENNIALS & BULBS

- *Angelica* species
- *Aquilegia* species
- *Digitalis* species (pictured)
- *Geranium sylvaticum*
- *Lilium* species
- *Lobelia cardinalis*
- *Nectaroscordum siculum*
- *Valeriana officinalis*
- *Verbascum* species
- *Verbena bonariensis*

⑥ Upright-growing perennials

Many of these are late summer- or autumn-flowering plants from North American prairie habitats. Others, such as *Thalictrum* species, flower earlier. Most go straight up, and if they are strong enough, their stems can act as a support for other plants. Some flop over, particularly on very fertile soils or in windy sites, and need staking, although modern varieties tend to be sturdier. In small gardens, limit the number of these plants, as they can overwhelm schemes and may also develop unattractive 'bare legs'.

UPRIGHT PERENNIALS & GRASSES

- *Achillea* species
- *Amsonia* species
- *Aster* species
- *Crocosmia* species
- *Echinacea* species
- *Eryngium* species (pictured)
- *Helenium* species
- *Monarda* species
- *Persicaria amplexicaulis*
- *Phlox* species
- *Solidago* species
- *Thalictrum* species
- *Veronicastrum virginicum*

Grasses:
- *Calamagrostis* x *acutiflora* 'Karl Foerster'
- *Miscanthus* species

⑦ Sub-shrubs

In nature, sub-shrubs grow intertwined with one another, but also with short grasses and perennials. The same effect can be achieved in the garden, with the strong proviso that they are *not* combined with taller perennials or those that tend to flop over them, as this can seriously affect their growth. Including the occasional sub-shrub can be very useful for winter presence or a nice solid bit of visual texture, although in very crowded borders it may be worth cutting back other plants around them.

SUB-SHRUBS

- *Cistus* species
- *Erica* species
- *Euphorbia characias* (pictured)
- *Hebe* species (smaller ones)
- *Helianthemum* species
- *Lavandula* species
- *Rosmarinus officinalis*
- *Salvia officinalis*
- *Santolina chamaecyparissus*
- *Teucrium chamaedrys*

⑧ Ground-hugging plants

The performance of individual species in this group depends on how many taller plants they can tolerate growing above them. Since they root as they spread, they are very useful for 'letting go', and work well when left to slowly infiltrate gaps and exploit the spaces between other plants. They are particularly effective at the front of plantings, where they can develop fully in the space they are given, and perhaps spill over the path or surface in front but also push backwards as much as they are able, or you allow.

GROUND-HUGGING PLANTS

- *Acaena* species
- *Ajuga* species
- *Bergenia* species
- *Campanula poscharskyana* and *C. portenschlagiana*
- *Liriope* species
- *Omphalodes* species
- *Persicaria affinis*
- *Thymus* species
- *Veronica* species (smaller ones)
- *Viola cornuta* (pictured)

CASE STUDY: Plant layering in a small garden

Design by Elsa Day

LEFT *Cordyline australis* 'Red Star' makes a distinctive focal point in an urban garden rich in plants. The coloured foliage of this and the *Robinia pseudoacacia* 'Frisia' behind, together with bold leaf shapes, dominate the upper and middle layers, with smaller, visually quieter plants filling in gaps at ground level. Many plants are in pots, which offer flexibility, particularly important in small gardens, and additional layering, allowing in-season plants to be emphasised, while hiding any that are past their best.

The owner of this small suburban garden, Elsa Day, is a self-confessed plantaholic, and plants do indeed dominate the design. About 20 years ago Elsa employed a garden designer to lay down a basic structure – important for plant collectors, as their hunger for different species tends to take precedence over design decisions.

As well as ornamentals, Elsa has included fruit trees, vegetables and herbs, and because she likes to shoehorn in new acquisitions, she is a champion of the layering technique. Shrubs, a few small trees, and climbers on the boundary walls create the upper level, below which are many perennials, then even smaller perennials, and finally low-level ground-cover plants lurk in corners and the tiny gaps most of us would not think to fill. ▶▶

PLANTING FEATURES

1. *Robinia pseudoacacia* 'Frisia'
2. *Choisya ternata* 'Sundance'
3. *Cordyline australis* 'Red Star'
4. *Miscanthus sinensis*
5. *Euphorbia characias* subsp *wulfenii*
6. *Hosta sieboldiana* variety
7. *Rheum palmatum*

GARDEN DIMENSIONS:
Approx 20m x 12m
(66ft x 39ft)

THE UPPER LAYER

THE MIDDLE LAYER

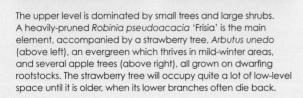

The upper level is dominated by small trees and large shrubs. A heavily-pruned *Robinia pseudoacacia* 'Frisia' is the main element, accompanied by a strawberry tree, *Arbutus unedo* (above left), an evergreen which thrives in mild-winter areas, and several apple trees (above right), all grown on dwarfing rootstocks. The strawberry tree will occupy quite a lot of low-level space until it is older, when its lower branches often die back.

A big *Hydrangea quercifolia* (above left) forms the centrepiece of the garden, and masks the view of the whole space, which helps to provide some level of mystery. Other elements that offer height, but take up very little ground space, are the obelisks supporting clematis (not shown). There are a few larger perennials, including *Echinops ritro* (above right), *Hemerocallis*, and a *Miscanthus* grass, all of which add mid-level bulk.

THE GROUND LAYER

FAR LEFT Perennials that self-seed, such as *Alchemilla mollis*, need ruthless weeding out or they will take over.

CENTRE *Ophiopogon planiscapus* 'Nigrescens' is a popular ground-level evergreen, but slow to grow.

LEFT Drought-tolerant annual poppies will self-seed in the gaps in paving in sunny areas.

The lower level is enhanced by the pebble and gravel surface. Gravel is a great choice of material, selectively promoting the germination of garden plants rather than weeds. Self-seeding by narrow plants is particularly useful here. These are annuals or biennials, like the Welsh poppy (*Meconopsis cambrica*) and love-in-the-mist, *Nigella damascena*, which squeeze into places where it would be almost impossible to sow them.

4

Plants for small gardens

Choosing plants

When selecting plants that will produce the layers seen in natural landscapes, look for a range of robust types that will be easy to care for, support biodiversity, and provide long-lasting colour and interest throughout the year.

Big plants for small spaces

In the last chapter we looked at how in nature different plant forms organise themselves into layers which can be replicated in a small garden. Here we look more closely at plant choices for each of the layers, including those that look good, perform well, reduce our workload, and support biodiversity.

Most people imagine that big plants will not suit a small garden. But wait! The late James van Sweden, one of the most influential garden designers of the 20th century, said that small plants make a garden feel even smaller, and many design professionals would agree. They may also quote the great design maxim 'less is more', stressing the graphic power of simplicity. I recall van Sweden's own tiny garden in Washington DC, which included just three big plants: a towering grass and two huge perennials. While they certainly made a harmonious composition, Mr van Sweden was a designer first, not a plantsman, and anyone who actually enjoyed gardening would have got very bored very quickly with such a scheme.

Another view, often expressed by Chinese and Japanese designers, is that the garden offers a vignette, a slice of another landscape, which transcends its physical limitations. By filling your outdoor space with plants, you are creating your own vignette by blurring its boundaries and including the diversity of a much larger landscape.

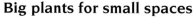

LEFT The foxglove, *Digitalis x mertonensis*, and fern, *Athyrium filix-femina*, in this lightly shaded town garden, along with hostas and a young Japanese maple, *Acer palmatum*, all benefit from the sheltered conditions. DESIGN BY CHRIS BEARDSHAW

TOP RIGHT Evergreen sedges, like the *Carex morrowii* 'Variegata' lining this path, offer year-round colour and texture. They are also slow-growing and easy to care for. DESIGN BY TOM BREKELMANS

CENTRE RIGHT A banana plant, *Musa basjoo*, dominates an exotic-style planting scheme,

a reminder that small city gardens often enjoy a surprisingly warm microclimate. DESIGN BY WAYNE AMIEL GARDEN

BOTTOM RIGHT The tree fern, *Dicksonia antarctica*, and shrub *Euphorbia mellifera*, are large plants that work well in small plots. DESIGN BY WAYNE AMIEL GARDEN

PREVIOUS PAGE The focus of this small garden is a purple plum, *Prunus cerasifera* 'Pissardii', with grasses and self-seeding species like the mauve *Verbena bonariensis* contributing to the gentle, naturalistic look. DESIGN BY ANNIE GUILFOYLE / NICKY PERKINS

Seasonal changes

Plants vary considerably in how well they perform throughout the different seasons. Evergreens tend to look respectable at all times, while most perennials have a definite season when they are at their best, after which they may be simply less interesting or look downright messy. In a large garden, plants can be hidden or attention drawn away from them during their off-season, but if you are the owner of a small plot you have no such luxury – your plants are on display at all times and your choices have to be more considered.

One solution is to select plants that never have an 'off' day, but if they are reliably tidy 365 days of the year, they tend to look boring after a while. Who wants to be surrounded with evergreens that look almost the same in winter as they do in the summer? Alternatively, you could include a succession of spectacular species, but fitting them all in may be a problem in a small space, and a garden dominated by these prima donnas risks being just as dull and looking worse than the evergreens as soon as the flowers are over. A flower-filled garden may also lack any sense of mass or structure, reducing its impact.

COMPARING PLANTS' SEASONAL PERFORMANCES FOR YEAR-ROUND COLOUR

This chart illustrates seasonal peaks and troughs in the performance of different types of plant and is designed to help you create year-round interest. Understanding that very few shrubs flower in late summer, for example, allows you to plan in something else close by for that time. Note also that 'early perennials' tend to be low and clump-forming, while late ones are nearly all larger and often upright, which means the planting in gardens that focus on bulbs and perennials, rather than shrubs, gets taller and bulkier as the year advances.

FLOWER INTEREST

SEED HEAD/ STRUCTURAL INTEREST, INCLUDING GRASS FLOWERING

FRESH FOLIAGE

DETERIORATING FOLIAGE

	Late Winter	Early Spring	Late Spring	Early Summer	Late Summer	Early Autumn	Late Autumn	Early Winter
SPRING BULBS								
EARLY PERENNIALS								
LATE PERENNIALS								
GRASSES								
ANNUALS								
SHRUBS								

Mix and match

The good news is that there are many possibilities in between these extremes. You can opt for flowers, but compromise and choose quieter beauties that offer longer seasons of interest. Designer Annie Guilfoyle recommends hardy geraniums, astrantias, grasses, and persicarias, which flower for weeks, even months, and do not flop or crowd out their neighbours. Carolien Barkman uses foliage plants, ferns, and species with big leaves, such as *Astilboides tabularis*, which looks great with sunlight filtering through its foliage. Carolien also stresses the importance of plants that self-seed and add a light, naturalistic touch to the design. Good examples of self-seeders include *Centranthus ruber*, aquilegias, thalictrums, and grasses, such as *Molinia*, which have a transparent, airy look.

> **"In a small garden, plants are on display all the time and choices must be considered carefully."**

OPPOSITE One of the joys of hydrangeas is the way that their old flowers remain on the plant, fading gracefully to provide many months of beautiful and sometimes unusual colours, like the antique shades of red exhibited by this *Hydrangea* 'Preziosa'. The heads can also be cut and dried for winter decoration.

BELOW LEFT AND RIGHT These images of the same garden viewed in spring and autumn show how colour and interest evolves throughout the year. In spring, the layered branches of white-flowered *Viburnum plicatum* 'Watanabe' dominate, while the purple-leaved *Cotinus coggygria* 'Royal Purple' makes an impact throughout the growing season. The white flowers in autumn are *Gaura lindheimeri,* which combine with the red grass *Imperata cylindrica* 'Rubra', yellow leaves of *Broussonetia papyrifera,* and tightly clipped box topiaries. DESIGN BY JACQUELINE VAN DER KLOET

Plants with staying power

The best way to create long-term interest in the garden is to concentrate on foliage and plants with good structure. Flowers are so often a ten-day wonder and it's best to think of them as the icing on the cake. You can ensure the garden always looks good, even if rather quiet for some of the time, by using leaves as your backdrop and inserting flowering plants as colourful extras. Use the following guidelines to construct a planting scheme that maintains interest throughout the year.

Repeat and long-term performers

The blooming period of flowering plants varies greatly. Some, such as irises, last just ten days or so, but many people enjoy this transience and the sense of passing seasons that such plants express. Most perennials will flower for several weeks, as do the majority of shrubs, but because perennials are generally much smaller in size, several can be fitted into the same area a single shrub would occupy. Their flowering season is more spread out, too – a large proportion of garden shrubs flower in spring, with few performing later in the year. Particularly useful are the perennials that repeat flower, with a main flush in early summer and another, though usually less floriferous, in autumn. The two performances are often encouraged by removing the faded flowers (known as dead-heading), but this is a small price to pay for another set of blooms.

One-season wonders

Often flowering for a long time, annuals are valuable additions to small-garden displays. While not all annuals flower repeatedly – once a poppy has stopped flowering, that's it – many bloom continuously, given sufficient moisture and nutrients. Perennials, which come up year after year, do not have the same biological imperative to keep on flowering.

The traditional mainstay of many gardens and parks, annuals and half-hardy perennials and bulbs fell out of fashion for many years, but they have enjoyed a revival in recent times, with looser, more natural-looking modern varieties that work well with perennials replacing old-style stiff, compact forms. Those from regions with mild

LONG-FLOWERING PERENNIALS

- *Achillea*, many varieties
- *Anaphalis* species
- *Aster x frikartii* (pictured), A. *pyrenaeus*, A. *thomsonii* 'Nanus'
- *Astrantia major* varieties
- *Echinacea purpurea* varieties
- *Persicaria amplexicaulis*
- *Verbena bonariensis*

REPEAT-FLOWERING PERENNIALS

- *Geranium endressii*, G. x oxonianum varieties
- *Nepeta* – many species (pictured)
- *Salvia nemorosa*; S. x superba; S. x sylvestris varieties
- *Viola cornuta*

LATE HALF-HARDY PERENNIALS

- *Dahlia* varieties
- *Diascia* varieties (pictured)
- *Heliotropium* species
- *Nemesia* species
- *Osteospermum* species
- *Penstemon* varieties
- *Salvia* (South American species)

winters and warm summers tend to flower late in cool summer climates, and may even survive the winter if it is not too cold (no lower than -10°C/14°F). Dahlias are good examples, as they are easy to grow, often survive the winter and flower exuberantly until the first frosts. With their intense colours and extravagant shapes, two or three can make a huge difference in a small space.

RIGHT The blue half-hardy *Salvia guaranitica* 'Blue Enigma', dark red buttons of *Knautia macedonica*, white *Dahlia* 'Nathalie's Wedding' and purple *Aster x frikartii* 'Mönch' produce this late season display. DESIGN BY LUMINE SWAGERMAN

Late-season blooms

It is easy to find plants that look good in early summer, but perennials and shrubs that flower several months later are invaluable. As well as filling this seasonal gap, perennials in this group also look tidy all summer long and tend to need less maintenance – see the diagram on p.80 – unlike earlier-flowering forms, which either look boring or messy after they have bloomed.

Late-flowering perennials

A good example of a planting design that depends on a grand finale is the herbaceous border. Packed with late-flowering perennials, annuals and tender sub-tropical species, these borders are very labour intensive and, as a result, went out of fashion for many years, but more recently there has been a resurgence of interest in the perennials they feature. Most are members of the hardy daisy family, vigorous and free-flowering, with an upright habit. Many also produce decorative seed heads and look good after flowering.

However, upright perennials have two disadvantages: the lower halves of their tall stems tend to look naked – the so-called 'bare legs' syndrome – and in windy or shaded areas, they often flop over. The first problem can be partly addressed by growing shorter plants in front of them, while staking, which is easy enough to do on a small scale, solves the second. Another solution for both problems is 'perennial pruning'. Many later-flowering perennials respond well to a gentle trim in late spring or early summer, which encourages them to bush out and produce shorter flowering stems. In some cases they will then bloom more profusely and, as they are smaller, the plants do not require as much staking.

Late-flowering shrubs

The most popular late-flowering shrubs are, of course, roses, which include varieties that bloom all summer or in flushes a month or so apart, but there are very few others to choose from. The majority of shrubs flower in spring, which allows time for their seed to grow and

LEFT *Hibiscus syriacus* 'Coelestis' is a good shrub for small gardens, as it has an upright, almost tree-like habit, and it is hardy but needs relatively high summer temperatures to flower well. It is also sometimes used for hedging, although this may reduce flowering.

COMPACT LATE-SEASON PERENNIALS

- *Agapanthus inapertus*
- *Ageratina altissima*
- *Aster divaricatus, A. dumosus, A. ericoides* varieties
- *Chelone* species
- *Chrysanthemum* species (pictured top left)
- *Crocosmia* species (pictured left)
- *Eurybia x herveyi*
- *Geranium procurrens*
- *Hesperantha coccinea*
- *Rudbeckia fulgida*
- *Salvia uliginosa*
- *Saxifraga fortunei* varieties
- *Sedum* – larger species, e.g. *S. spectabile*
- *Symphyotrichum lateriflorum* var *horizontalis* cultivars
- *Tricyrtis* species

LATE-FLOWERING SHRUBS

- *Abelia* species
- *Abutilon* species
- *Buddleja davidii* varieties, and some other *Buddleja*
- *Ceanothus* 'A.T.Johnson', *C.* 'Autumnal Blue', *C.* 'Burkwoodii', *C. impressus*
- *Escallonia* species
- *Fuchsia* species (pictured third from top)
- *Hebe* – many varieties
- *Hydrangea* varieties
- *Lavatera x clementii*
- *Phygelius* varieties
- *Potentilla fruticosa* (pictured left)

ripen before autumn. So while it is tempting to fill your garden with beautiful shrubs in spring, you will then have to endure dull masses of greenery for the rest of the year. However, there are a few later-flowering types, and by including one or two, you can inject colour just when it is needed.

MASTERCLASS
TWO-SEASON PLANTS

Many plants offer two seasons of interest, combining both attractive flowers and good quality foliage. A wide range also produces flowers followed by decorative seed heads or colourful berries. The table below outlines some of the best examples and will help you to choose plants that have this two-season advantage.

Seed heads for winter interest
Plants whose flowers are followed by attractive fruit or seed heads are very useful in smaller spaces. Some shrubs produce colourful berries, and many perennials offer ornamental seed heads, some of which disintegrate as temperatures fall, while others stand until the end of the winter, maintaining their structure, even after small birds have eaten the seeds. Grasses are a good example of plants that provide this type of winter structure.

The play of winter light is important in appreciating seed heads, particularly grasses, which are ideally seen backlit against a darker background. The effect is especially pronounced in regions with low winter sun, where the light brings to life subtle tonal variations in the browns, fawns and yellows of the dead foliage too. Also consider the scale of each plant's seed heads and foliage. Those that make an impact from a distance are best in a larger garden, but the exquisite detail and small-scale beauty of some plants can only be appreciated close-to, and these are ideal for the edges of paths or patios in compact spaces.

TWO-SEASON PERFORMERS

The plants in this chart put on a good performance twice a year, offering great garden value and lots of interest in a small space. Most flower and then produce colourful or interesting seed heads or berries several months later. Others may offer evergreen or very early foliage with decorative fruit later in the year.

Legend: FOLIAGE · FLOWER · BERRIES · SEED HEAD · AUTUMN FOLIAGE

		Late Winter	Early Spring	Spring	Late Spring	Early Summer	Mid Summer	Late Summer	Autumn	Early Winter
SHRUB	Amelanchier canadensis			■					■	
PERENNIAL	Amsonia species				■				■	
PERENNIAL	Arum italicum 'Pictum'	■						■		
CLIMBER	Clematis 'Bill MacKenzie'							■	■	
PERENNIAL	Hosta plantaginea				■			■		
PERENNIAL	Iris foetidissima	■	■	■	■				■	■
PERENNIAL	Iris sibirica			■	■				■	■
PERENNIAL	Lunaria rediviva			■	■	■			■	■
SMALL TREE	Malus – crab apples				■			■	■	■
PERENNIAL	Phlomis russeliana				■	■			■	■
SMALL TREE	Prunus 'Ukon'				■				■	
PERENNIAL	Pulmonaria – silver leaf types		■	■						
SHRUB	Rosa 'Fru Dagmar Hastrup'					■			■	■
BIENNIAL	Verbascum nigrum					■	■	■	■	
SHRUB	Viburnum opulus				■				■	

ABOVE The seed heads of the grass *Pennisetum alopecuroides* provide a decorative feature well into the winter and contrast beautifully with the dark heads of *Sedum* 'Matrona', and fluffy *Clematis* 'Bill MacKenzie'. DESIGN BY JACQUELINE VAN DER KLOET

PERENNIALS AND BULBS WITH GOOD SEED HEADS

- *Actaea* species
- *Agastache rugosa*
- *Allium* species – larger 'drumstick' varieties
- *Echinacea* species (pictured left)
- *Eryngium* species
- *Geum triflorum*
- *Iris foetidissima, I. sibirica*
- *Lunaria rediviva*
- *Phlomis russeliana*
- *Pulsatilla vulgaris*
- *Sedum* – larger species

SMALL TREES AND SHRUBS WITH COLOURFUL FRUIT

- *Callicarpa bodinieri*
- *Cotoneaster* species
- *Crataegus* species
- *Malus* species
- *Pyracantha* varieties
- *Rosa* species and varieties with single flowers
- *Sorbus* species
- *Viburnum opulus*

CLIMBERS WITH GOOD SEED HEADS

- *Clematis* 'Bill MacKenzie'
- *Schisandra* species

ANNUALS (A) AND BIENNIALS (B) WITH GOOD SEED HEADS

- *Amaranthus* species (A)
- *Briza maxima* (A)
- *Digitalis ferruginea* (B)
- *Dipsacus fullonum* (B)
- *Fibigia clypeata* (A)
- *Hordeum jubatum* (A)
- *Lagurus ovatus* (A)
- *Lunaria annua* (A)
- *Nigella* species (A)
- *Papaver somniferum* (A)
- *Phacelia tanacetifolia* (A)
- *Scabiosa stellata* (A)
- *Verbascum nigrum* (B)

Focus on foliage

Decorative foliage is the bedrock of many successful planting designs. The leaves of a good foliage plant may be large or glossy, have an interesting shape, texture or colour, or they may be light and feathery, or elegantly arranged on the branch. Anything out of the ordinary that attracts the eye may be worth including.

As with seed heads, scale plays an important role in small spaces. Intricate details or texture on the leaves, their arrangement on the stem, the way they look in

the light – these aspects of foliage can be all too easily lost in the larger garden but are appreciated close-to, and make up part of the small garden aesthetic. Large-leaved plants also have a particular value in the small garden and selecting just a few with real grandeur can have a powerful effect. This is more easily achieved with large-leaved perennials or coppiced or pollarded woody plants (see p.48) than with a tree, simply because they are easier to control.

Finally, include foliage plants for early and late colour. In areas with mild winters, some perennials make early growth in spring, while a few perennials, as well as trees and shrubs, turn fiery shades in autumn.

LEFT The dark, dramatic evergreen leaves of *Helleborus foetidus* are always valuable, while the clipped hawthorn, *Crataegus monogyna*, will make a leafy dome in summer. DESIGN BY JACQUELINE VAN DER KLOET

PERENNIALS WITH EARLY FOLIAGE

- *Acanthus* species
- *Arum italicum* (pictured)
- *Cynara cardunculus*
- *Geranium*, most species
- *Mathiasella bupleuroides*

PERENNIALS WITH ELEGANT FOLIAGE

- *Aruncus dioicus* 'Kneiffii'
- *Dicentra* species (pictured)
- *Gillenia trifoliata*
- *Hosta* varieties
- *Kirengeshoma palmata*
- *Sanguisorba* species
- *Selinum* species
- *Thalictrum* species
- *Veratrum* species

PERENNIALS AND GRASSES WITH AUTUMN COLOUR

- *Amsonia* species
- *Ceratostigma* species. (pictured)
- *Geranium soboliferum*
- *Panicum virgatum*, some cultivars, e.g. 'Shenandoah'
- *Schizachyrium scoparium*

PERENNIALS WITH LARGE LEAVES

- *Astilbe rivularis*
- *Blechnum chilense*
- *Darmera peltata*
- *Hosta sieboldiana*
- *Rheum* species (pictured)
- *Rodgersia* species

SHRUBS AND SMALL TREES WITH AUTUMN COLOUR
(those with B also have very attractive bark)

- *Acer campestre*, *A. griseum* **B**, *A. palmatum*
- *Amelanchier* species
- *Aronia* species
- *Berberis thunbergii*
- *Cotinus coggygria*
- *Crataegus* 'Autumn Glory'
- *Enkianthus* species (pictured)
- *Fothergilla* species
- *Malus tschonoskii*
- *Mespilus germanica*
- *Prunus* – Japanese cherries, and *P. sargentii*, *P. serrula* **B**
- *Rhus typhina*
- *Ribes odoratum*
- *Sassafras albidum*
- *Sorbus* species
- *Stewartia* **B** (pictured left)

Using colourful leaves

Leaves that are not green stand out simply because they are different. There are many plants that have colourful foliage, including purple-, silver-, and yellow-leaved forms. Variegated foliage is another option and can be effective when used sparingly.

Adding coloured foliage to a garden immediately creates interest, but too much can be wearing, especially if you include a spectrum of different hues. Variegated plants in particular do not mix well, so keep them apart or set them against plain-leaved partners. Also use those with cream, yellow or white variegation in shady areas to inject light. Silver and grey foliage plants combine well with those of a similar hue. Most are also evergreen and produce beautiful effects in sunny gardens in winter, while in spring, they make a good backdrop for colourful bulbs, especially those with mauve, purple, and blue flowers.

Colours also affect perspective: dark shades recede, while pale or bright hues visually jump forward. So if you want to make the back of a short garden seem further away, use dark foliage at the rear to create the illusion of a longer distance. Bright or variegated foliage will make the distance seem closer. Use the examples on pp.92–93 to make your choices.

ABOVE An essay in silver, this *Stachys byzantina* 'Big Ears' and *Santolina chamaecyparissus* are both evergreen.

RIGHT *Cotinus coggygria* 'Royal Purple' forms a large deciduous shrub which can be pruned to size or shaped.
DESIGN BY JACQUELINE VAN DER KLOET

HOW FOLIAGE COLOUR AFFECTS PERSPECTIVE

This chart shows how leaf colours can be dark or light, with green at the midpoint, although, of course, there are pale and dark greens too. Plants with darker foliage colours recede in perspective terms, while those with lighter coloured leaves leap forward visually and foreshorten the perspective. 'Gold' and 'silver' variegation (or, more accurately, 'yellow' and 'white') helps to introduce light into shady areas.

DARKEST	DARK	←→	LIGHT	LIGHTEST
purple	bronze	green	yellow-green	silver
purple-black	red		gold	silver variegation
	brown		grey	
			golden variegation	

Purple and dark foliage

Some plants naturally have purple foliage, but in most cases, the deep purple coloration is the result of a mutation. A fair number of shrubs and perennials sport leaves in this rich shade, which contrasts well with brighter colours.

PURPLE-, BRONZE/ BROWN-, AND BLACK- LEAVED PLANTS

SMALL TREES AND SHRUBS

- *Acer palmatum*, many varieties
- *Berberis thunbergii*, many varieties
- *Cercis canadensis* 'Forest Pansy'
- *Corylus maxima* 'Purpurea'
- *Cotinus coggygria* 'Royal Purple' (pictured top left)
- *Ilex x meserveae*
- *Photinia* species – spring foliage only (pictured second from top)
- *Physocarpus opulifolius* 'Diabolo'
- *Pieris* species – spring foliage only
- *Prunus cerasifera* 'Nigra', *P. x cistena*

PERENNIALS

- *Actaea racemosa* – several varieties
- *Ajuga* – many varieties
- *Astilbe* – many varieties
- *Heuchera* – many varieties (pictured third from top)
- *Ligularia dentata*
- *Rodgersia* varieties
- *Salvia officinalis* 'Purpurascens'
- *Sedum telephium* – many varieties

GRASSES

- *Carex* – many species have bronze or brown foliage, e.g. *C. comans*, *C. flagellifera*, and *C. testacea*
- *Imperata cylindrica* (pictured bottom left)
- *Ophiopogon planiscapus* 'Nigrescens'
- *Uncinia rubra*

Yellow and gold-variegated foliage

Usually the result of a mutation, which tends to slow down growth, variegated and yellow-foliage plants are often smaller than the plain-leaved species. Such plants are sometimes more sensitive to light, too, and thrive in light shade.

GOLDEN VARIEGATION, OR YELLOW FOLIAGE

SMALL TREES, SHRUBS AND SUB-SHRUBS

- *Calluna vulgaris* varieties
- *Catalpa bignonioides* 'Aurea'
- *Elaeagnus x ebbingei*, *E. pungens* varieties
- *Euonymus fortunei* (pictured top left) and *E. japonicus* varieties
- *Fuchsia* 'Golden Treasure'
- *Griselinia littoralis* 'Dixon's Cream'
- *Hebe ochracea* 'James Stirling'
- *Ilex aquifolium* 'Golden Queen' (pictured second from top)
- *Ligustrum ovalifolium* varieties
- *Philadelphus coronarius* 'Aureus'
- *Salvia officinalis* 'Icterina'
- *Spiraea japonica* 'Goldflame', *S. japonica* 'Golden Princess'

PERENNIALS

- *Hosta* – many varieties (pictured third from top)
- *Symphytum x uplandicum* 'Axminster Gold'
- *Vinca minor* 'Argenteovariegata'

GRASSES

- *Carex elata* 'Aurea'
- *Hakonechloa macra* 'Aureola'
- *Miscanthus sinensis* 'Gold Bar' and 'Little Zebra' (pictured bottom left)

Silver and grey foliage

Silver- or grey-leaved plants have evolved to survive in hot, dry climates, such as the Mediterranean region. The colour helps reflect light and protects the foliage from drying out. Most plants with silver or grey leaves are sub-shrubs, of which lavender (*Lavandula*) is the best known, although there are some shrubs and perennials too. Many are also evergreen, and a few have soft leaves. Silver variegation, like the gold type, is a result of a mutation rather than climate adaptation.

SILVER-WHITE VARIEGATION

SMALL TREES, SHRUBS AND CLIMBERS

- *Actinidia kolomikta* (pictured left)
- *Cornus alternifolia* 'Argentea'
- *Euonymus fortunei* (pictured second from top) and *E. japonicus*, many varieties
- *Ilex aquifolium* 'Argentea Marginata'
- *Ligustrum ovalifolium* varieties
- *Rhamnus alaternus* 'Argenteovariegata'

PERENNIALS

- *Astrantia major* 'Sunningdale Variegated'
- *Brunnera macrophylla* – many varieties (pictured third from top)
- *Hosta* – many varieties
- *Iris pallida* 'Variegata'
- *Phlox paniculata* 'Norah Leigh'
- *Pulmonaria* species (some varieties)

GRASSES

- *Arundo donax* var *versicolor*
- *Calamagrostis* x *acutiflora* 'Overdam'
- *Carex* – many varieties (pictured bottom left)
- *Miscanthus sinensis* 'Morning Light' and 'Rigoletto'

SILVER AND GREY FOLIAGE

SMALL TREES AND SHRUBS

- *Pyrus salicifolia* 'Pendula'
- *Salix exigua*, *S. lanata*, *S. repens* var *argentea*

SUB-SHRUBS

- *Atriplex halimus*
- *Ballota pseudodictamnus*
- *Cistus* species
- *Convolvulus cneorum* (pictured top left)
- *Coronilla valentina* subsp *glauca*
- *Hebe* 'Pewter Dome', 'Red Edge', and many more
- *Helichrysum italicum* subsp *serotinum*, *H. petiolare* (pictured second from top)
- *Lavandula* species (pictured third from top)
- *Ruta graveolens*
- *Salvia officinalis*
- *Santolina chamaecyparissus*

PERENNIALS

- *Anaphalis* species
- *Anthemis punctata* subsp *cupaniana*
- *Artemisia stelleriana*
- *Hosta sieboldiana* (note – this needs damp soil)

GRASSES

- *Festuca glauca* (pictured bottom left)
- *Helictotrichon sempervirens*
- *Koeleria glauca*
- *Poa labillardieri*

Choosing evergreens

Evergreens have been valued by all gardening cultures for centuries. Today, with every garden centre offering a wide variety, it is difficult to imagine what it was like for our ancestors, for whom, in cooler regions at any rate, there were very few. Nearly all the evergreens for gardens are conifers or shrubs with dark, often glossy, leaves. Both bring winter cheer, but seen all year round, they can become boring or depressing, which is why most people prefer to grow just a few, or to clip them into topiary. Evergreen plants fall into several categories.

Conifers

These are botanically different to flowering plants (they do not have flowers), and have evolved to survive stressful environments. Most are too large for small gardens, but some are very narrow and fit in well. So-called 'dwarf' conifers are extremely useful for those who garden in regions with very cold winters, although remember that most are, in fact, slow-growing rather than dwarf and may become surprisingly large in time.

Evergreen shrubs

Large-leaved evergreen shrubs tend to come from climates with moderate or high rainfall and mild winters; in other words they do not like drought, low temperatures or cold or strong winds. They are of limited value in small gardens beyond the odd carefully chosen and well-placed specimen.

Smaller-leaved evergreen shrubs often hail from slightly stressful habitats, such as woodlands, or rocky or exposed terrain. They tend to grow slowly, have a dense branching habit and are relatively resilient. Crucially, many are happy in some shade, and a good number also tolerate clipping (see pp. 50–51).

Sub-shrubs

Ideal for small gardens, the great advantage of evergreen sub-shrubs is that they do not present the flat, hard, light-reflecting glare that many larger-leaved evergreens exhibit, or the louring effect of those with dark green leaves. This is partly down to their small size, but also because their dense foliage creates a matt effect, which is easier on the eye. The fact that many have silver-grey foliage is another advantage. Good examples are Hebe cupressoides, rosemary (Rosmarinus officinalis) and all those listed under silver/grey foliage shrubs on p.93.

Evergreen climbers

Not many evergreen climbers survive temperate climates year-round, apart from the ivies that make up the Hedera genus, but these have a reputation for running rampant; they need regular pruning if they are not to overwhelm houses or cover windows. If you have time to provide annual maintenance, then they can be regarded as first-rate and self-repairing cladding, as their leaves will throw water off the house and help to shelter it from the cold and wind. Ivies creep up walls using tiny aerial roots, and do not need support. In regions with mild winters, the choice of evergreen climbers expands rapidly (see opposite and p.117).

Evergreen perennials

There are very few truly evergreen perennials. Most simply keep their leaves through the winter, replacing them annually in spring; in hard winters some may lose their foliage as temperatures fall. Nevertheless, those with overwintering leaves are valuable, as they are the right scale for small gardens and offer a wide variety of shapes, colours, and textures.

Low-level evergreens

In the last chapter we saw how low-level creeping plants create interest at ground level and complete our layers of plant structure. Another advantage is that a high proportion of these diminutive plants are evergreen. This is because many are from stressful environments where it is an advantage to use all available light to grow at any time of year. Many also have attractive colourful foliage.

These low-level plants grow in various ways: some have one central stem linking the top growth to the roots, while others root as they creep along. The latter are of most use as they spread more easily and they also recover from damage because every part of the plant has its own network of roots.

CONIFERS

- *Abies koreana* 'Silberlocke'
- *Chamaecyparis lawsoniana* – dwarf forms (pictured left)
- *Cryptomeria japonica* 'Vilmoriniana'
- *Picea mariana* 'Nana'
- *Taxus baccata* 'Standishii'
- *Thuja occidentalis* 'Rheingold'

EVERGREEN SHRUBS

- *Baccharis* species
- *Berberis darwinii, B. linearifolia, B. microphylla*
- *Bupleurum fruticosum*
- *Buxus* species
- *Ceanothus* species
- *Choisya* species
- *Cotoneaster* species
- *Hebe* species
- *Ilex* species
- *Laurus nobilis* (pictured bottom left)
- *Lonicera nitida*
- *Mahonia* species
- *Myrtus communis*
- *Nandina domestica*
- *Pieris* species
- *Pittosporum tenuifolium*
- *Prunus lusitanica* (pictured second from top)
- *Pyracantha* species
- *Rhododendron* – many species are small with dense, twiggy growth, the most widely sold are the types often called 'Japanese azaleas' but there are many more
- *Skimmia japonica*
- *Teucrium fruticans*
- *Viburnum davidii, V. tinus*
- Many listed under golden variegation or yellow foliage' (p.92) and silver/white variegation' (p.93)

EVERGREEN SUB-SHRUBS

- *Hebe cupressoides,* and many more
- *Rosmarinus officinalis* (pictured)
- Plus, all those listed under Silver/grey foliage shrubs (see p.93)

EVERGREEN CLIMBERS

- *Clematis armandii*
- *Dregea sinensis* *
- *Hedera helix*
- *Hedera hibernica* (pictured)
- *Holboellia coriacea* *
- *Trachelospermum jasminoides*

* not reliably hardy below -6°C (21°F)

EVERGREEN PERENNIALS

- *Bergenia* species
- *Epimedium* species – some are semi-evergreen, some deciduous
- *Euphorbia amygdaloides* var *robbiae*
- *Euphorbia characias*
- *Helleborus* species
- *Heuchera* varieties, in mild winters only
- *Liriope* and *Ophiopogon* species
- *Phlomis russeliana*
- *Vinca* species (pictured)

LOW-GROWING PLANTS WITH EVERGREEN OR SEMI-EVERGREEN FOLIAGE

Many of these will tolerate occasional stepping on

- *Acaena* species
- *Achillea* – small species
- *Ajuga* species (pictured)
- *Armeria* species
- *Cotula* species
- *Erinus alpinus*
- *Hypsela reniformis*
- *Linaria alpina*
- *Mazus* species
- *Mentha requienii*
- *Potentilla* – some small species, e.g. *P. aurea* and *P. alba*
- *Pratia* species
- *Prunella* species
- *Sedum* – small-growing species
- *Thymus* – creeping types

Including structure

Structure in a plant is an important design quality but difficult to define. Perhaps the best way to decide whether or not a plant has structure is to look at it in black and white. Taking a photograph of your border and then turning it into black and white also helps you to assess the structural content of the planting scheme as a whole – many colourful borders will look like porridge when viewed in this way!

We have seen how clipping can create structure but many other plants can be said to have good structure, including those with distinctive or large leaves, an interesting branching pattern, or a strong clear shape, which makes them stand out from their neighbours. Another set of structural plants are the exotics, but it is really only feasible to include them year-round in locations with a very mild climate.

Structure through the seasons

The key to designing a small garden, structure is essential, but how much should you include? This is a very personal decision. Some people like the drama of big plants, spiky shapes, and eye-catching leaves; others find this look makes them feel restless. It may help to think about how much drama you wish to inject: do you want a bold dynamic planting mix, a graphic but more restful look, or would you rather sacrifice structure for shorter-lived floral effects?

The other consideration here is time. Some plants always show off their fine bones; others, such as large-leaved perennials, reveal their structure for a shorter period, or, as very often happens, collapse into a tatty mess once they have flowered. We can think about structure and seasonal interest on a gradient ranging from 'dramatic' to 'weak', and from long season to short. The chart on pp.98–99 shows how this works.

RIGHT The upright flower spikes of *Lythrum salicaria* 'Robert' and the *Kniphofia* add structure to this border, while *Penstemon* 'Rich Ruby' injects a frill of long-lasting colour in the foreground.
DESIGN BY GARDENS OF APPELTERN

OPPOSITE The perennial *Sanguisorba tenuifolia* 'White Tanna' (right) has an intriguing shape and structure; its divided leaves also appear in spring, offering interest before it flowers in late summer.
DESIGN BY LEEN GOEDEGEBUURE

WOODY STRUCTURAL PLANTS

- *Aralia elata*
- *Cornus alternifolia,*
  C. controversa
- *Fatsia japonica*
- *Juniperus scopulorum*
  'Skyrocket'
- *Mahonia* species
  (pictured)

PERENNIAL STRUCTURAL PLANTS

- *Cynara cardunculus*
- *Dierama* species (pictured)
- *Echinops* species
- *Eryngium* species
- *Iris sibirica*
- *Kniphofia* varieties
- *Libertia* species
- *Limonium platyphyllum*
- *Lythrum* species
- *Polygonatum* species
- *Thalictrum* species
- *Veronicastrum* varieties

MASTERCLASS
PLANTS' STRUCTURE OVER TIME

This simple chart plots the strength of plants' structure, from dramatic at the top, down to weak at the bottom, and the length of time those plants can be relied on to offer that structure. This is a good way of determining which plants offer the best structure and for how long. The following examples show in more detail how to interpret and use the information in the chart.

Dramatic structure through the seasons
(Examples shown at the top of the chart):

- *Allium giganteum* is very dramatic, flowering for nearly a month in early summer. Its seed heads also look good for a while, but then tend to break up, so it has great structure for about three months.
- *Acanthus spinosus* has elegant foliage and a big flower spike which stands for a while, but looks increasingly untidy over time. The plant has good structure for between three and six months.
- *Calamagrostis* 'Karl Foerster' is an ornamental grass that flowers in early summer and has beautiful seed heads which look good until late winter. It offers structure for six to nine months of the year.
- *Yucca filamentosa* is an evergreen, and looks almost identical from one month to another, providing year-round structure and interest.

Weak structure through the seasons
(Examples shown at the bottom of the chart):

- *Geranium pratense* forms a neat clump of foliage, flowers in early summer and then falls over, looking a mess for the rest of the year.
- *Geranium endressii* tends to do the same but produces a second set of flowers in late summer, offering weak structure for three to six months of the year.
- *Epimedium* has nice glossy foliage, but it is low-level and does not contribute much structure. It is semi-evergreen but often develops a 'bad hair day' look in winter; nevertheless, it can contribute to the garden structure a little for up to nine months each year.
- *Liriope* is similar to *Epimedium*, with good but not very dramatic strappy foliage, but it is truly evergreen and never has an off day. It can be relied upon to contribute a little structure to the front of a border year-round.

.

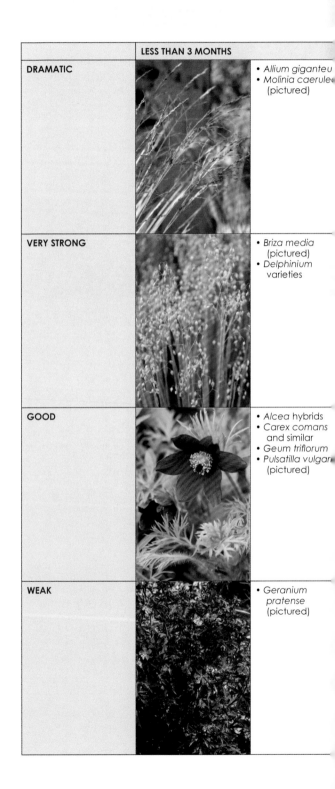

	LESS THAN 3 MONTHS	
DRAMATIC		• *Allium giganteu* • *Molinia caerule* (pictured)
VERY STRONG		• *Briza media* (pictured) • *Delphinium* varieties
GOOD		• *Alcea* hybrids • *Carex comans* and similar • *Geum triflorum* • *Pulsatilla vulgar* (pictured)
WEAK		• *Geranium* *pratense* (pictured)

3–6 MONTHS	6–9 MONTHS	MORE THAN 9 MONTHS
• Acanthus spinosus (pictured) • Cynara cardunculus • Miscanthus sinensis	• Aralia elata • Calamagrostis x acutiflora 'Karl Foerster' (pictured), C. x acutiflora 'Overdam' • Stipa gigantea	• Juniperus scopulorum 'Skyrocket' (pictured) • Mahonia x media 'Charity' • Yucca filamentosa
• Achillea species • Baptisia australis (pictured) • Darmera peltata • Echinacea purpurea • Kirengeshoma palmata • Panicum virgatum • Pennisetum alopecuroides • Polygonatum species • Selinum wallichianum • Thalictrum species	• Chionochloa conspicua • Hakonechloa macra • Kniphofia varieties • Molinia caerulea • Perovskia atriplicifolia • Phlomis russelliana • Rodgersia varieties • Sanguisorba species (pictured) • Sedum spectabile, S. telephium varieties • Verbacscum nigrum • Veronicastrum varieties	• Polystichum setiferum (pictured) • Rosmarinus officinalis • Stipa tenuissima • Verbascum bombyciferum
• Agapanthus varieties • Agastache rugosa • Astilbe varieties • Calamagrostis brachytricha • Digitalis species (pictured) • Euphorbia characias • Limonium platyphyllum • Lythrum species • Persicaria amplexicaulis • Sporobolus heterolepis • Verbena bonariensis	• Alchemilla mollis (pictured) • Crocosmia species • Dierama species • Hosta varieties • Libertia species	• Bergenia species • Buxus sempervirens (pictured) • Helleborus x hybridus • Iris foetidissima
• Geranium endressii (pictured) • Hemerocallis varieties	• Epimedium species (pictured)	• Hebe – smaller species • Liriope muscari (pictured) • Vinca species

Designing with grasses and grass-like plants

Using grasses and other grass-like plants, such as sedges (*Carex* species) and wood rushes (*Luzula* species) in garden schemes is a relatively new idea. While many grasses are too big or spread too rapidly for a small garden setting, there is a range of compact species and smaller-growing varieties of the larger forms that are ideal. The great advantage of grasses is their long season of interest, most contributing colour and texture from late spring to autumn, with many also featuring sturdy seed heads that carry on looking good through winter.

For small gardens, choose from the following two loosely defined groups of grasses.

Seed-head grasses

Grown primarily for their flowers and similar-looking seed heads, these grasses perform from mid- or late summer to mid- or late winter. There are a few very large ones, some of which paradoxically work surprisingly well in small gardens; they may be 2 metres (7ft) tall, but most of that is air. With far-flung panicles shooting out from a relatively short, non-spreading basal clump of leaves, they take up little ground space but make a big impact. Lower-growing grasses can offer wonderful displays of denser, fluffy seed heads at knee height.

Foliage grasses

Many grasses and sedges are now being promoted as small, long-season foliage plants, their neat tufts of linear leaves providing a low-key presence and foil for larger or showier plants. Ideal for small gardens, some are fresh green, others blue-grey, and a few come in various shades of bronzy brown, introducing a whole palette of subtle colours. These grasses have either a tufted habit, or grow to form slowly spreading mats.

LEFT *Calamintha nepeta* 'Blue Cloud' and *Salvia nemorosa* 'Caradonna' with the grass *Calamagrostis* x *acutiflora* 'Overdam'.

BIG, BUT AIRY, GRASSES FOR SMALL GARDENS

- *Chionochloa conspicua*
- *Molinia caerulea* subsp *arundinacea* (pictured)
- *Stipa calamagrostis*
- *Stipa gigantea*

MEDIUM-SIZED GRASSES WITH GOOD STRUCTURE

- *Calamagrostis* x *acutiflora* 'Karl Foerster' and 'Overdam'
- *Calamagrostis brachytricha*
- *Miscanthus* 'Elfin'
- *Miscanthus sinensis* 'Gracillimus Nanus', 'Little Kitten', 'Nippon', 'Yakushima Dwarf' (pictured)
- *Molinia caerulea* (not *arundinacea* varieties)

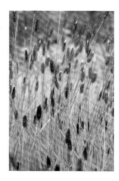

SMALL GRASSES WITH INTERESTING FLOWERS AND SEED HEADS

- *Bouteloua gracilis*
- *Briza media*
- *Pennisetum* species (pictured)
- *Sporobolus heterolepis*
- *Stipa tenuissima*

SMALLER FOLIAGE GRASSES AND GRASS-LIKE PLANTS

- *Acorus* species
- *Carex* species (pictured)
- *Festuca* varieties
- *Hakonechloa macra*
- *Liriope* species
- *Sesleria* species
- *Uncinia rubra*

Introducing scent

Creating a garden full of perfumed plants is perhaps something that the small city garden can achieve more easily than a suburban or country garden, its walls creating the perfect environment for floral or foliage scents to be both released and trapped. It is one thing going up to a flower to smell it, another to have the scent wafting up as soon as you step out of the back door.

Criticism is often levelled at the nursery industry for growing or breeding flowering plant varieties that lack scent. This is true to some extent, as visual impact is the most marketable – it is not possible to attach a representation of a scent to a catalogue or press release. If fragrance is something that particularly interests you, it may be necessary to do a little extra research and track down varieties that perform really well.

Many of the best scented plants have white or pale blooms, as they have evolved to focus their energies on scent rather than colour. Species that are pollinated primarily by moths are also more likely to be fragrant in the evening and at night, and they tend to be white or light in colour too; examples include honeysuckles (*Lonicera* species) and jasmines (*Jasminum* species). Red and orange flowers are usually the least fragrant, as these colours attract pollinating birds, which do not have a good sense of smell.

Fragrant foliage

Aromatic foliage has the advantage over floral scents in that its season is longer. Many aromatics, but by no means all, are Mediterranean plants; their leaves contain scented oils that reduce desiccation and deter predators. The combined fragrance of *Cistus*, lavender, sage, and other Mediterranean herbal aromatics is a particularly strong reminder of the power of scent to evoke memories. However, many plants release their fragrance only when the leaves are agitated, so plant them close to pathways where you will brush against the foliage.

TOP LEFT Sweet peas are famous for their fragrance, but varieties need to be researched carefully, as not all have a strong scent.

LEFT Honeysuckle, *Lonicera periclymenum*, is an easy-to-grow climber; its sweet scent is best in the evening, when it attracts moths.

PLANTS WITH GOOD FLORAL SCENTS

- *Buddleja davidii*
- *Convallaria majalis*
- *Daphne* species (pictured top)
- *Dianthus* varieties (pictured second left)
- *Elaeagnus pungens*
- *Erysimum cheiri*
- *Euphorbia mellifera*
- *Hamamelis mollis*
- *Jasminum* species
- *Lathyrus odoratus*
- *Lilium* – only trumpet- or funnel-shaped flowers, *L. regale* is the best
- *Lonicera* – only those with white or yellow flowers
- *Mahonia*, especially *M. x media* 'Charity'
- *Narcissus*: multi-headed Tazetta types, flat-faced, usually white Poeticus types, and the Jonquil group
- *Osmanthus* species
- *Rhododendron* – deciduous azalea types
- *Rosa* – 'old fashioned' roses are very good, and the modern 'English Rose' class, or smell before you buy!
- *Trachelospermum* species
- *Viburnum x bodnantense* (pictured left), *V. x burkwoodii*, *V. x carlcephalum*
- *Viola odorata*

AROMATIC-LEAVED PLANTS

- *Aloysia citrodora* (pictured)
- *Artemisia abrotanum*
- *Cistus* species
- *Hyssopus officinalis aristatus*
- *Lavandula* species
- *Lindera benzoin*
- *Mentha* species
- *Myrtus communis*
- *Rosmarinus officinalis*
- *Salvia* species
- *Satureja* species

TOP RIGHT The flowers of *Clematis recta* 'Purpurea' have a vanilla scent.

RIGHT *Osmanthus x burkwoodii* is an evergreen shrub whose spring flowers have a powerful fragrance. It can also be used for hedging.

Cultivating the exotic look – tropicalismo!

Urban gardens may be small but they have a great advantage over sites in the country. Cities tend to be warmer and often enjoy sheltered microclimates. As a result, a south-facing urban garden will be a sun trap and have a longer growing season and a milder climate than one a few miles away in the suburbs.

Many gardeners exploit this benefit by growing plants, such as olives and some palms, that would not be hardy in less sheltered areas in their region. Exotic plants like these can create the sense of a place far away, offering the opportunity for some horticulture-led escapism and the spinning of fantasies. And in a city or town, they also provide one of the most effective ways of transcending the urban jungle.

Getting the look

While some creators of exotic gardens focus on foliage, others are drawn to the colourful floral exuberance of warm-climate plants, although even in these gardens, foliage should still be the backbone, adding visual mass as the flowers come and go. The classic blooms for this tropicalismo look, such as salvias, cannas and dahlias, also tend to perform late in the summer and therefore need a structural base for the rest of the year.

Successful exotic-looking gardens are those that combine a number of different elements.

- **Plants that look exotic, but are actually hardy,** including those with large or dramatic spiky leaves, or foliage with a rosette shape. Examples include many yuccas, and *Rodgersia* species.
- **Species on the edge of their hardiness zone** that will grow in a sheltered city environment. The downside is that if unprotected these plants may die during a very cold winter. Examples include palms, tree ferns, and hardy bananas.
- **Plants that are not quite hardy but survive outside with some added protection.** Some gardeners go

> **"In a town or city, exotic plants provide an effective way of transcending the urban jungle."**

to great lengths to protect plants with plastic or straw wrapping. In many cases, if the top growth is killed off by frost, the roots survive and the plant regenerates from the base. Examples could be those in the previous category, but in a colder climate.

- **Species that are hardy in dry climates**, but will rot in winter wet. Many are from deserts where it may get very cold but never wet. Grow them in very free-draining soil and cover with a transparent material in winter. Examples include agaves and cacti.
- **Tender plants** that are planted out in the ground or in pots for the summer, and brought back inside in winter. Many house plants cope with this treatment, and in some cases are healthier, as they suffer fewer attacks from pests and diseases. Examples include *Schefflera*, tropical figs, warm-climate palms.
- **Annuals that grow rapidly during the summer** but die in the autumn. These are particularly useful for adding splashes of colour. Examples include *Ricinus communis* and French marigolds (*Tagetes*).
- **Bulbs and tubers**, which die down in the winter and can be lifted, dried and stored indoors until late spring. Examples include cannas and dahlias.

LEFT The tropical look is particularly suited to city gardens, creating a sense of fantasy and offering the warmer conditions the plants need
DESIGN BY WAYNE AMIEL

RIGHT This bronze-leaved canna (left) will need winter protection in cold areas; *Crocosmia* 'Lucifer' (right) looks tropical but it is hardy.

CASE STUDY: A plant-packed small garden
Design by Joanne Bernstein

FAR LEFT Texture, foliage forms, repetition, and rhythm are the key design elements used to create this style of perennial planting. A very tactile garden due to the plants, which soften the hard landscaping materials and sharp geometry.

TOP LEFT Measuring about 2m (7ft) long and 3m (10ft) wide, this paved terrace is just large enough to comfortably fit a dining table and chairs. It has a very slight slope away from the house to enable drainage, and is surrounded by planting, allowing the diners to view flowers and foliage at close range.

BOTTOM LEFT The perennials and grasses in this garden are not the very tallest, which would visually overwhelm and, crucially, look out of proportion here, but short to medium-sized species, or those with a sideways dimension, as well as an upright one.

Designer Joanne Bernstein has created her garden using combinations of perennials and ornamental grasses. An average town garden with a distinctly contemporary look, it features an off-centre path that crosses a lawn and borders. A central bed serves to mask the end of the plot and maximises the impact of the plants, which have been designed to be seen from a large window at the rear of the house.

The plants include a modern range of easy-care, long-lived, late-performing species. "The shade at the back makes a good backdrop for perennials, winter stems and grasses," says Joanne. Most of the plants are cut down in early spring, when the garden is comparatively bare, but as the year progresses the garden disappears beneath the foliage and flowers.

The pale yellow *Achillea* 'Mondpagode', a relatively new and reliable hybrid of a genus that is often not long-lived in the garden, is combined here with orange *Helenium* 'Moerheim Beauty' and the grass *Deschampsia cespitosa*. The latter adds a delicate touch in late summer and autumn, and forms a tussock that combines well with flowering perennials, both practically and visually.

Eryngium giganteum, known affectionately as Miss Willmott's ghost, is a biennial with very good structure, which is retained through the winter. To survive in the garden long-term it needs to self-seed – however, as many gardeners, including Joanne, have discovered, it can do this a little too enthusiastically and the plant can become a weed. If this is a problem, choose a perennial *Eryngium* instead.

DESIGN FEATURES

1. Terrace
2. Mixed border with grasses
3. Lawn
4. Stepping stones
5. Border planting
6. West-facing terrace for evening dining
7. *Soleirolia* 'lawn'
8. Shady planting area under existing trees, with hidden compost bins

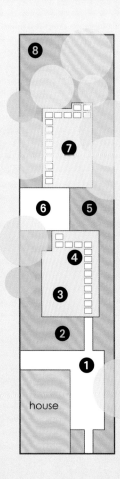

GARDEN DIMENSIONS: Approx 25m x 8m (82ft x 26ft)

107

Vertical planting

Climbing high

Wrapping your garden with flowers and foliage, climbing plants help to increase the layering effect and are ideal for small gardens, taking up very little ground space while offering a wide variety of colourful and seasonal effects.

> "When selecting a climber, check the plant label carefully for its eventual size."

Extend your planting area

In small gardens, the boundaries surrounding your property offer an additional opportunity to increase the flower and foliage cover, and in some cases, they may even provide more space than the ground area itself. For example, a garden ten metres long and six metres wide will have a total surface area of 60 square metres, but if the boundary fence or wall is two metres high along three sides, you will also have 52 square metres of vertical surface, plus some of the house wall. You can use this area for climbing plants, as well as shrubs and a few trees, known collectively as 'wall shrubs', which can be trained against the boundaries to green your surroundings in a way that ground-limited plants can never do.

When selecting a climber, check the plant label carefully for its eventual size. Sorry to be bossy, but if you have a small garden, you have to choose with care, since large climbers have an annoying tendency to reach out and cling on to anything they can, and an overgrown climber can be very difficult to rein in.

The height given for a climber is the size it will reach at maturity, so if you have a two-metre (7ft) fence, a two-metre (7ft) climber should grow no further than the top, while a three-metre (10ft) plant will run along it a little, but a five-metre (16ft) plant may be too big. Some large climbers can be trained along the tops of fences, and will produce spectacular results if you have the time to tie them in and prune them: the pink-flowered *Clematis montana* is a good example, or the Japanese vine, *Vitis coignetiae*, with its vivid autumn colour. When planting large climbers, remember that you also need to know who and what is on the other side of the fence, as you may have no control over the plant when it reaches over.

The house itself also offers an opportunity to grow a large climber. A wisteria, rose or large-leaved foliage plant reaching up to the top of a two-storey building is a magnificent sight, but for plants that are not self-clinging (see pp.112–113), you will need to install specially-designed fixings and support systems. Also consider the maintenance required before committing to a high-reaching climber; be prepared to scale a ladder or call in experts to prune it regularly.

ABOVE 'Bobbie James' is a rambler-type rose which can potentially grow very large, making it ideal for covering or screening anything you may wish to hide.

OPPOSITE Wisteria is a most rewarding climber, although the flowering season is relatively short (just a few weeks) and it requires rigorous pruning. Train it over a pergola or up a wall on strong supports as the stems become very heavy.
DESIGN BY ADAM FROST

PREVIOUS PAGE Grape vines clamber up supports, lending this garden a vertical dimension as well as conveying hints of the Mediterranean, where overhead shading is all-important. Here, the support structures are open, as this is in England where too much shade would not be welcome.
DESIGN BY ELSPETH THOMPSON

GARY PUBLIC LIBRARY

MASTERCLASS
HOW PLANTS CLIMB

Some plants have evolved to climb as a way of reaching the light without the need for strong supporting stems, while others have sturdier growth and simply grow tall enough to reach above their neighbours. Most climbers use one of the following mechanisms to scramble up, and by identifying the method your chosen plant uses, you can determine whether or not it will need artificial support, and if it does, what type would be the most suitable.

> **"By identifying the method your chosen plant uses to climb, you can determine whether or not it will need an artificial support."**

Self-clinging climbers

These plants attach themselves to vertical surfaces, including trees, by means of tiny aerial roots. Their great advantage is that they do not need any kind of support system, but the ability to cling unaided can also lead to problems since *they* decide where they are going to grow and need to be cut back regularly – in a small or town garden this may be an important issue if you wish to maintain good relationships with neighbours.

There is a widespread belief that self-clinging climbers, such as ivy, damage buildings, but research has shown that this is not true; on the contrary, these climbers can help to protect the skin of the building, rather like a self-repairing cladding system, as long as the mortar is sound.

There are not many self-clinging climbers for cool climates: ivies (*Hedera* species) and the Boston ivy/Virginia creeper group (*Parthenocissus* species – pictured) are the most common options and both are grown for their foliage rather than for flowers or fruit.

Tendril climbers

Many climbers have evolved mechanisms, usually adaptations of leaves, which stretch out and fix onto anything within grasping distance. Because the grasp of these plants is quite small and they are more free-ranging in their habits than twiners (see opposite), they are best grown on a system of wires or trellis that offers both horizontal and vertical support – if you keep on top of them, they are relatively easy to train in the direction you want them to grow.

Tendril climbers are dominated by the enormous and wondrous genus, clematis (pictured). There is a vast array of both species and hybrids available to gardeners, and while some are enormous, others are more manageable in size, and there are also small-growing varieties for container use. In addition, we must not forget the passion flowers (*Passiflora*), especially in warmer climates, and vines (*Vitis*), although the latter can potentially grow very large where conditions are favourable.

Thorny climbers

The rose climbing around the door is a chocolate box cliché, but its thorny stems can turn it into one of the most dangerous plants in the garden, should an untied stem start lashing about in a high wind.

Climbing roses have stiff stems and need to be directed and tied onto a sturdy support, or you can allow them to scramble through trees, where their thorns help them cling onto the bark. Rambling roses tend to be larger than the climbers, although the flowers are often smaller, and they are best grown through a tree or over a pergola. Once established, ramblers will scramble through a tree's canopy to reach the light at the top, producing an impressive display in early summer.

Wall shrubs

These may be lax-growing shrubs that need something to lean on, or shrubs that require the protection of a warm sunny wall, or those that can be pruned so they lie flat against a vertical surface. *Ceanothus* species are good examples of shrubs that can be grown in this way, and in cold areas they also benefit from the shelter of a wall or fence; they do, however, need to be tied onto trellis fixed to the vertical surface and pruned annually to keep them in place. Other examples include *Pyracantha*, *Garrya elliptica*, *Abutilon* species, *Magnolia grandiflora*, *Prunus* (apricot and peach) varieties, and some *Cotoneaster* species, such as C. *horizontalis*.

Twining climbers

The stems of these climbing plants wind themselves around a support. They need vertical wires, slender posts or other uprights to support them, and sometimes have to be persuaded to grow horizontally. Some are very large, notably the *Wisteria* species, but most are suitable for the smaller garden, particularly the honeysuckles (*Lonicera*) and the jasmines (*Jasminum*). The flexible stems of honeysuckles are easy to deal with, but jasmines can be slightly difficult because they tend to form unruly masses of stiff stems – pruning can help keep them in line.

Right climber, right place

The great thing about climbers and wall shrubs is that you can fit so many into a small space. As well as plants growing on a restricted footprint, you can space climbers relatively close together and allow them to mingle as they clamber up their support systems. However, there are some provisos. One is that the soil must be deep enough for the plants to develop a normal root run; where the soil is shallow or full of rubble, plant options may be limited to those that can tolerate these conditions, such as *Ceanothus*. Or you could plant in raised beds to increase the depth of soil.

Another factor to consider is that climbers grown together will compete with one another, and occasional intervention will be required to keep the peace, cutting back the most vigorous to provide more space for the less competitive plants.

BELOW The vigorous vine relative, *Vitis coignetiae*, will need to be kept in check by training and pruning. However, it performs very well if trained horizontally, like this one clambering along the wall. DESIGN BY ELSPETH THOMPSON

Check the aspect

The way in which your wall or fence faces is especially important when choosing a spot for climbers because the extremes of the environment are emphasised here: a sunny vertical surface will be hotter than anywhere else in the garden, while one facing away from the sun will be in shade practically all of the time.

A sunny wall can be a fantastic place for climbers, allowing you to grow plants that may be less than fully hardy elsewhere. The range of climbers broadens in warmer climates, where many more evergreen or heavily scented species thrive. A sunny wall, a few climbers, a small terrace, some pots of flowers... and the Mediterranean beckons.

Shaded walls or fences present more problems and if the surface faces north, then little other than ivy is likely to succeed. In partial shade, species of clematis, honeysuckle and *Parthenocissus* will be happy if there is direct sunshine for at least half the day. In shadier sites, they will always be stretching towards the light.

The honeysuckle, *Lonicera x brownii* 'Dropmore Scarlet' will potentially grow up to 4m (13ft), and it is semi-evergreen, a great advantage for clothing small garden boundaries and features. Like all climbing honeysuckles it twines, which means that it requires quite minimal support and will, for example, climb into a small tree with little persuasion.

Clematis armandii, with its large evergreen leaves, is a real 'tropicalismo' plant (see p.105), but despite its exotic looks, it is surprisingly hardy. Early spring sees a profuse display of scented white flowers over several weeks. It tends to run towards the top of its support and may require training to grow sideways. The lower leaves may also die off and need disguising.

The story behind the naming of the blue passion flower, *Passiflora caerulea*, by 16th century Catholic missionaries is a fascinating one, laden with religious symbolism (hence the name). It is slightly tender and will thrive on trellis fixed to a sunny brick wall or fence. Large orange-coloured edible (although not very tasty) fruits appear after the flowers.

Wisteria grows very large, very quickly once established, and using it to dress up a house can be rewarding but hard work! Wisterias need ruthless pruning and cutting back annually to a central framework – 90 per cent of the growth may need to be removed in any one year. Such control will also help it flower from a young age.

USING CLIMBERS AS DIVIDERS

If you are looking to create a leafy garden screen, such as a coulisse (p.22), to divide up a small space, climbers offer the perfect solution. Trellis fixed between two fence posts and covered with flowering climbing plants makes an effective and attractive screen, while taking up little ground space. Not as wide as a hedge, climbers rarely block out the light completely and exert less competition on plants growing nearby, allowing a richer planting mix. To lengthen the flowering season, combine two or three climbers on one panel.

Since many climbers have a strong tendency to grow upwards, rather than across, it may be necessary to train the stems horizontally. In doing so, you will also encourage the plant to send up new shoots from multiple points along the horizontal stems, resulting in a more prolific flower display. This is particularly true of roses, but other climbers also respond well to this form of training.

BELOW *Rosa* 'Climbing Iceberg' grows to around 4m (13ft) and the flowers make a good partner for the feathery plumes of the tall perennial *Aruncus dioicus*.
DESIGN BY GARDENS OF APPELTERN

The hop, *Humulus lupulus*, is an unusual climber in that it is herbaceous and dies down in winter, which makes it a really good summer screening plant for free-standing trellis where a winter presence is not required. The dried flowers have traditionally been used for indoor decorations. *H. lupulus* 'Aureus' has yellow-green leaves.

Climbing roses are popular but caution is needed if you plan to grow one, as they vary enormously in size. The good news is that some are small enough for the average-sized fence. They also grow very successfully through trees, where they scramble among the branches and emerge to flower in the sun.

Selecting foliage over flowers

When making plant choices, it is all too easy to get carried away and choose them for their flowers alone, but remember it is the leaves that you will be looking at for most of the year and, given the angle of walls and fences, those leaves will be looking right at you.

Choosing climbers with beautiful foliage makes sense. There are relatively few reliably hardy evergreens – ivies include a wide range but offer no flowers to speak of, while *Clematis armandii* is exceptional, with large evergreen leaves and attractive flowers. However, there are plenty of deciduous climbers with attractive foliage, a few of which are among the best sources of autumn colour, particularly *Parthenocissus*.

RECOMMENDED CLIMBERS FOR FOLIAGE

All examples, except the *Vitis*, are either medium-sized, manageable, or slow-growing enough not to run away with you. If you like *Vitis*, it can be ruthlessly pruned to keep it in check.

- *Akebia quinata*
- *Clematis armandii*
- *Hydrangea petiolaris* (pictured below left)
- *Itea ilicifolia* (wall shrub)
- *Laurus nobilis* (wall shrub)
- *Myrtus communis* (wall shrub – pictured below right)
- *Pileostegia viburnoides*
- *Schisandra grandiflora*
- *Trachelospermum* species
- *Vitis* species

LEFT A golden hop (*Humulus lupulus* 'Aureus') clambers up a wooden pergola, which will support several climber species.
DESIGN BY SUSAN SHARKEY

CLIMBERS FOR CONTAINERS

If you have a garden with very little soil, you may have to restrict your climbers to containers. They will perform as well (or as badly!) in pots as any other plant, but the size of the vessel will limit their ability to grow; it is probably unrealistic to expect a containerised climber to reach more than two or three metres (7–10ft). However, many of the smaller clematis and honeysuckle varieties are successful in pots and, indeed, some have been bred with container-growing in mind. One of the benefits of restricting plant growth in pots is that it allows you to limit the size of desirable large species, such as vines, wisteria, or even the big and rangy kiwi fruit (*Actinidia chinensis*), but whether you choose large or small climbers, be prepared to water and feed them regularly to keep them in good condition – an automatic watering system is a wise investment for a roof terrace or extensive range of containerised plants.

BELOW Honeysuckle, a decorative vine and sweet peas are joined here by white-flowered *Trachelospermum jasminoides*, one of the best climbers for sheltered town gardens.
DESIGN BY ELSPETH THOMPSON

Trailing and flowing effects

As well as training climbers *up*, it is sometimes possible to allow them to trail *down*. If there is a situation where you can plant on top of a retaining wall, then climbers can be allowed to flow over it, although the drop must not exceed the maximum height of the plant. This technique works well for species with soft and flexible growth, such as Boston ivy and Virginia creepers (*Parthenocissus* species), clematis and ivies.

Retaining walls can also sometimes offer the opportunity to plant non-climbing plants in the gaps and holes. Many smaller perennials, particularly those sold for rockeries or as 'alpines', will flourish in such a situation, especially if there is sun for at least a few hours of the day. Some species, such as aubrietia, dwarf perennial wallflowers (*Erysimum*) and *Helianthemum* will form dense clumps that seemingly flow out of the wall.

GREEN WALL SYSTEMS

There are many vertical planting or 'green wall' systems now available that offer lush and varied planting, based on high-quality foliage plants growing on a suspended framework. These can be very effective but most need to be attached to a water and power supply. They can also require quite a lot of maintenance, but for situations that are used intensively, particularly for entertaining, such as a courtyard or terrace, they provide a wonderful talking point.

Plants that form spreading clumps or have low creeping stems are the best choices for green walls. Heucheras and hostas, which thrive naturally on wet cliff faces, do particularly well. Evergreens, including *Bergenia*, *Liriope* and *Ophiopogon* can be successful too, while *Carex* and *Luzula,* and the smaller clump-forming grasses will also be happy on a wall. Combine plants with different leaf colours, textures, sizes and shapes to produce a tapestry effect – about six different species will create contrast without looking too bitty. Hardiness is vital, as vertical plantings are prone to freezing.

BELOW A beech hedge acts in a similar way to a green wall and increases privacy in a city garden. Beech has the advantage of retaining its dead brown leaves through winter. DESIGN BY ZAKI & RUTH ELIA

BELOW This green wall is planted with hostas, ferns, and *Lamium maculatum* 'Beacon Silver', creating a good balance of foliage colours, sizes and shapes.

RIGHT Different varieties of ivy (*Hedera helix*) form a textured screen in a contemporary courtyard garden. Ivy is a vigorous plant and will need careful management to keep it in check. DESIGN BY TON VISSERS

6

Mini wildlife havens

Small sanctuaries

Birds, small mammals, amphibians and beneficial insects can all find homes in our gardens, and research shows that even tiny urban spaces can play an important role in increasing biodiversity and providing habitats for wildlife.

"When grouped together, small gardens can provide a habitat of rare complexity and richness."

Catering for wildlife

In a world that is increasingly urbanised and where rural areas are dominated by the intensive farming needed to feed growing populations, gardens have a major role to play in wildlife conservation. Study after study shows how gardens support more biodiversity than many areas of countryside – even where no special effort is made to include a wide range of plants and wildlife features.

A small garden may provide only a limited amount of space, but the accumulated area of many urban plots can together add up to a great deal, and provide a habitat of rare complexity and richness. How to make a small garden contribute to biodiversity is not difficult, but it helps to understand some basic ecology first.

Wild plants and animals are linked together in a complex nutritional web, known as the 'food chain'. At the bottom are vast numbers of tiny invertebrates, mostly unseen, that feed on plants or plant litter. They provide food for larger invertebrates, chiefly insects and spiders, which in turn are eaten by birds and mammals. These may then be eaten by carnivores, like foxes or hawks. And, of course, cats, although these are not a 'natural' part of the chain.

Although most of us are only really aware of the upper, larger, and more visible part of the food chain – the birds in the garden and the occasional fox, for example – without the invisible army of toiling and chewing invertebrates, there would be very little wildlife for us to enjoy. So when creating habitats in the garden, we have to consider each level of the food chain, and ensure that we provide food and shelter for all the creatures listed above. This may sound complicated but, in fact, it boils down to providing just a few key features.

All wildlife has three basic needs:
- **A place to roost**, where creatures can be secure; a 'home' from which forays for feeding and breeding can be made.
- **Sources of food** which, in the case of some insects, may be different for the larvae and adults.
- **Places to nest**, breed, and produce the next generation.

ABOVE Rhododendron flowers illustrate the complexities of nature, as their nectar can actually be poisonous to domestic honey bees, but not to wild bumblebees, which are drawn to them in large numbers.

OPPOSITE A single-flowered white rambler rose has been encouraged to grow into a tree. Climbers like roses can give a second life to a tree which is failing or even dead, and provide a habitat for birds and insects.
DESIGN BY WILLEM TIMMERMANS & TOM POSTMA

PREVIOUS PAGE The planting in this relaxed informal garden, with its conventional family lawn and borders along the boundaries, illustrates perfectly the principle of tree/shrub/perennial layering that creates a range of good habitats for wildlife.
DESIGN BY CAROLIEN BARKMAN

Nurturing environments

The basic needs of wildlife are met by different types of environment and, more specifically, by different plants and planting combinations. To understand how planting and the garden-as-habitat affects wildlife, it helps to 'think like a bug'. A small insect needs somewhere to feed and to be safe; once exposed – for example, when crawling up a tree trunk or scurrying across bare ground – it is vulnerable to a sharp-eyed bird or watchful shrew. 'Thinking like a bug' involves considering not just what you are going to eat, but where you are going to eat it, and how you are going to get across from one place to another in safety.

Creating corridors

The example of the bug shows the importance of providing cover for wildlife, while the box opposite identifies how you can achieve this and also the ways in which complexity and variation in planting will enrich your wildlife habitat. Another important factor to consider is the 'connection' you forge between those areas of planting, so that trees brush against shrubs, perennials are adjacent to the shrubs, and shorter perennials are beneath the taller ones.

Connections are, of course, very similar to the concept of layering introduced in Chapter 3 (pp.40–75) and they are also linked to the concept of 'wildlife corridors'. Wildlife requires safe routes that link protected areas and allow creatures to move from place to place unharmed. In the garden, we need to create mini-corridors between different micro-habitats to produce the same effect on a small scale.

We see our garden as our domain. We know its physical and other limits, but wildlife does not recognise our legal property boundaries and sees only habitat. However, what it might find are walls and

TOP LEFT This garden offers a rich variety of habitats, with plants of different types and sizes creating continuity between one another. Flowers and seed heads, such as the alliums, provide food too.
DESIGN BY ELSPETH THOMPSON

BOTTOM LEFT Long grass and annual flowers look attractive in summer and early autumn, and provide a different habitat to lawns and borders. However, they can look untidy when the flowering is over and may need to be disguised with other plants.
DESIGN BY SOUTHEND-ON-SEA BOROUGH COUNCIL

"Wildlife does not recognise our legal property boundaries and sees only habitat."

EASY WAYS TO PROVIDE SHELTER

Cover, or physical shelter, is very important if you want to provide the best conditions for the small invertebrates that make up the invisible bulk at the bottom of the food chain (see p.123). Traditional garden styles tend to minimise cover; naturalistic planting, on the other hand, provides more of it.

The physical make-up of the planting in your garden is important for enhancing garden biodiversity. Here is a quick check-list of good and bad environments for wildlife.

BAD FOR WILDLIFE
- Trees emerging directly out of grass
- Mown lawn between paving or hard surfaces
- Bare earth or bare mulch between plants
- Uniform-sized plants
- Hard surfaces
- Limited variation
- An absence of shrubs

fences that restrict access, and, more crucially, gaps in habitat. The kind of connections, or mini wildlife corridors, we create between trees, shrubs and perennials, can be thought of as potentially extending to the entire neighbourhood, and it is worthwhile talking to your neighbours and considering how good habitats in your garden can be linked to the habitats in theirs.

Wildlife neighbourhoods
As a general rule, people tend to have less well-tended areas at the end of their garden; there are often more trees and big shrubs here too. This may mean that those in adjacent properties link up across the boundary at this point, making a good connection for wildlife. You can also leave gaps under a fence or have a more open, picket-style or chain-link fence that allows creatures to pass through easily from one side to the other.

GOOD, OR BETTER, FOR WILDLIFE
- Trees adjacent to shrubs, with climbers connecting them
- Perennials grown alongside shrubs
- Small areas of mown lawn between borders
- Plants growing so close that there is little bare earth visible in between
- Leaf litter on soil surface
- Wide variation in plant size and type
- Organic mulches
- Wide variety of planting styles and features

ABOVE Layers of shrubs, and large and smaller perennials, provide a dense network of habitats, as well as visual richness. Dense planting allows for species that flower or look good at different times to mingle, providing a long-lasting effect.
DESIGN BY DAN PEARSON

Providing water

Building a garden pond, even a small one, can vastly increase the range of wildlife in the garden, attracting amphibians, aquatic insects and, of course, larger wildlife that feeds on them. The pond does not need to be deep; more important is how it is connected to the rest of the garden.

Make a gentle slope on one side of your pond so that animals, such as frogs, can get out after having jumped in (amphibians can actually drown if they are trapped in the water). Also include cover and connection with planting on one or more sides, ensuring that the plants come right up to the water's edge and perhaps overhang it a little. Provide additional cover and flowers for insects with marginal plants set into the water around the edges of the pond, or create a mini-wetland filled with bog plants between the water and borders.

CREATING A SMALL POND

A small garden pond is easy to make with a flexible butyl liner. Dig a hole with gently sloping sides and shelves around the edges to create different depths. This is important because different water levels support different plant types. Marginals, which live in the shallow water at the edge of a pond, are particularly important, as they help to create a natural effect and also allow wildlife to access the water. Once the hole is ready, carefully inspect the base and remove any sharp stones or other rubble that may damage the liner; old carpet or purpose-made cushioning material should also be laid beneath the liner to help protect it. Once filled with water, place aquatics like water lilies at the bottom and marginals on the shelves around the edges.

FAR LEFT To be useful, and safe for wildlife, garden pond edges must be sloped to allow wildlife to access the water easily. Gravel or other loose material also provides places for invertebrates to hide under if necessary.
DESIGN BY WILSON MCWILLIAM

LEFT The dense planting towards the back of this pond provides good cover for wildlife, such as frogs and toads.
DESIGN BY WILLEM TIMMERMANS & TOM POSTMA

Selecting plants for wildlife

We have established that growing a wide variety of plants helps to increase biodiversity. Nature thrives on variety, which is excellent news for gardeners who want to attract wildlife and like lots of different plants, but not such good news for those who like the simplicity of graphic minimalism.

While larger plants, and shrubs in particular, may offer roosting and nesting sites, it is a plant's role as a food source which is of most importance to wildlife. Sometimes, of course, this may be a negative factor – for example, when caterpillars strip foliage or slugs bite holes out of leaves – but unlike gardeners of the past, many people today are more relaxed about minor plant damage. A garden with a rich and varied array of plantlife can also visually absorb more nibbled or marked leaves than a formally planted one. This is because a wide selection of plants, designed in naturalistic layers, will conceal the impact of a damaged plant here and there better than gardens set out in a traditional style. Another benefit of choosing a greater number of plant varieties is that pests (and diseases) tend to focus on particular species, so including a rich mix spreads the risk of damage.

BEST PLANTS FOR BIODIVERSITY

From the vast choice of plants now available, what are the best ones to choose for biodiversity? Try to include a few from each of the following categories in your garden. Specific examples are given opposite and on pp.130–131.

① Native plants

② Flowers for pollinators

③ Berries

④ Seed heads

⑤ 'Weeds'

⑥ Aquatics and bog plants

BELOW LEFT *Perovskia* 'Blue Spire' and *Achillea filipendulina* 'Parker's Variety' are both good plant choices for pollinating insects and will thrive in hot dry locations. The colours and plant shapes also complement one another, and make an eye-catching combination.

BELOW RIGHT *Echinacea purpurea* 'Magnus' is a 'two-season' plant for wildlife, as the flowers feed honey bees and butterflies and, several months later, the seed heads are pecked open by finches.

① Native plants

There is a vociferous body of opinion which claims that only natives are good for wildlife and, by implication, non-natives are bad. However, the scientific evidence simply does not support this view, although there may be good reasons for including a few natives. This is because some insect larvae, those of butterflies and moths in particular, are very picky about the plant species they eat. This issue varies in importance from region to region, so do a little research on native plants with real value for wildlife in your area.

EXAMPLES OF NATIVE PLANTS FOR NORTHERN EUROPE

- *Achillea millefolium* (pictured below)
- *Aruncus dioicus*
- *Centaurea scabiosa*
- *Filipendula ulmaria*
- *Hedera helix*
- *Knautia arvensis*
- *Leucanthemum vulgare*
- *Origanum vulgare*
- *Prunella vulgaris*
- *Senecio ovatus*
- *Silene dioica*
- *Succisa pratensis*
- *Trifolium pratense*

EXAMPLES OF NATIVE PLANTS FOR NORTH AMERICA

- *Asclepias* species
- *Aster lateriflorus*
- *Echinacea* species
- *Eupatorium* species
- *Monarda* species
- *Penstemon* species
- *Phlox* species
- *Solidago caesia*
- *Symphyotrichum* species (formerly *Aster*)
- *Tiarella* species

② Flowers for pollinators

If you spend some time watching insects visiting flowers you will soon see how some blooms will only be visited by large wild bees, and never by the sleeker honey bees, while others seem to attract only flies or wasps. The following general indicators show what attracts whom:

- Large flowers and asymmetrical blooms attract wild bees, especially bumblebees.
- Small, shallow flowers packed into tight heads are favoured by honey bees, wild honey bees, and butterflies.
- White flowers with strong night-time scent attract moths.
- Red or orange tubular flowers lure hummingbirds (if you live in the Americas).
- Double flowers – attract nothing! Double flowers are mutants, which in nature would not function, as insects cannot get access to their nectar and pollinate them.

EXAMPLES OF FLOWERS FOR POLLINATORS

- *Calendula officinalis*
- *Cotoneaster* species
- *Origanum* species (pictured below)
- *Ribes sanguineum*
- *Solidago* species
- *Symphytum* species
- *Verbena bonariensis*

③ Berries

Trees and shrubs with berries are a great winter resource for birds, so choose a range of fruits that ripen at different times to extend the harvest. Birds also prefer certain colours, notably red, and species that produce these colourful berries, such as *Amelanchier*, will be stripped very early. Pyracanthas and hawthorns will not become palatable until frosted, which means that no wildlife will eat them until later in the winter – an arrangement that suits everybody, as we want berries to look at, and birds are particularly vulnerable to starvation as winter progresses.

EXAMPLES OF BERRIED PLANTS

- *Amelanchier* species
- *Aronia* species
- *Cotoneaster* species
- *Crataegus* species (hawthorn – pictured below)
- *Euonymus europaeus*
- *Hedera helix*
- *Ilex* species
- *Prunus avium*
- *Rosa* species (not double garden roses)
- *Taxus baccata*
- *Viburnum opulus*

④ Seed heads

Some birds eat berries, others eat seeds. Perennials with tall seed heads can attract flocks of seed-eating birds, providing a burst of entertainment for the garden owner, before they move off to pastures new. Such plants may harbour insect larvae in their seed heads too, providing yet another source of food for birds.

EXAMPLES OF PLANTS WITH SEED HEADS

- *Alcea* hybrids
- *Amaranthus* species
- *Betula* species
- *Centaurea* species
- *Chasmanthium latifolium* (pictured below)
- *Clematis orientalis*
- *Dipsacus fullonum*
- *Echinacea purpurea*
- *Echinops* species
- *Helianthus* species
- *Monarda* species
- *Phlomis russeliana*
- *Salvia nemorosa* and related species
- *Solidago* species
- *Verbena bonariensis*

⑤ 'Weeds'

As the well-known saying goes, a weed is a plant in the wrong place. Gardeners today tend to be more relaxed about uninvited 'guests' in the garden, but it is important to distinguish between benign species and aggressive colonisers – something every gardener has to learn by trial and error. Benign species are those little plants that seem to grow in every garden which, because they are short, are easily out-competed and do not seed too enthusiastically. They can play their role in creating biodiverse habitats, and often provide cover for invertebrates, as well as offering a food source. Many are so minor that we can forget about them a lot of the time.

EXAMPLES OF BENIGN WEEDS

- *Allium ursinum* (pictured below)
- *Anagallis arvensis* (scarlet pimpernel)
- *Bellis perennis* (lawn daisy)
- *Chenopodium* species (fat hen)
- *Euphorbia peplus* (petty spurge)
- *Prunella vulgaris* (selfheal)
- *Trifolium* species (clovers)
- *Veronica persica* (Persian speedwell)

⑥ Bog plants and aquatics

Choosing aquatic plants is a little problematic, as many natives are extremely vigorous and can fill a small pond in no time, so research sizes carefully. However, some, such as the sculptural horsetails (*Equisetum*), can be restrained if they are grown in pots to stop them spreading. There are several different levels in a pond (see p.127), each of which supports a particular range of plants, so it is important that you choose the right plant for the water depth available. Nearly all die down in winter, but in some cases they leave behind attractive seed heads.

EXAMPLES OF AQUATICS AND BOG PLANTS FOR SMALL PONDS

- *Butomus umbellatus*
- *Caltha palustris*
- *Equisetum hyemale*
- *Houttuynia cordata* 'Chameleon'
- *Iris sibirica, I. versicolor* and *I. laevigata* (pictured below)
- *Menyanthes trifoliata*
- *Nymphaea*, dwarf varieties
- *Typha minima*

Wildlife-friendly garden features

So-called 'wildlife gardening' has been the most important new horticultural movement of recent decades. Inevitably, it has been followed and partly promoted by suppliers of associated products, including bumblebee hotels, hedgehog houses, bird boxes, and bird feeders. While bird tables and bird and bat boxes can really make a difference, there is, as yet, little evidence that much thoughtfully-provided accommodation is used by insect guests.

Far more important is ensuring that your garden is wildlife friendly and includes plant-packed, multi-layered borders, and different types of habitat. The following ideas, some of which make beautiful garden features in their own right, will serve wildlife much better than most bought goods.

- **Make a mini-meadow** Leave a small area – a square metre (39in) or so – of uncut lawn, or only cut it occasionally, to provide a little bit of extra habitat for insects and small creatures.
- **Leave woodpiles** Heaps of twigs and logs left to moulder away in a quiet area of the garden will provide habitat and a food source for invertebrates.
- **Include drystone retaining walls** Walls made of loose, unmortared stones can make a high quality wildlife habitat, although they can also provide hiding places for slugs and snails.
- **Plant trees** Research has shown that trees, more than almost any other feature, significantly increase garden biodiversity, although the reasons for this are not fully understood. So think very carefully before removing or trimming a tree; if it is casting too much shade, remove the lower limbs to allow in more light instead of cutting it down. Alternatively, some species may be pollarded (see pp.48–49)
- **Don't pull up every weed** As we have seen, you can live with some benign weeds (see p.131).
- **Find space for a compost heap** This will be a habitat in its own right.
- **Don't throw everything on the compost heap** Weeds, dead flowers, and small prunings can be thrust in among growing plants to decay out of sight, forming micro-habitats as they do so.
- **Monitor insect infestations** Not all infestations are undesirable. For example, the aphids that afflict *Thalictrum* in early summer are unsightly close-to, but they are invisible from a distance, and are eaten by birds as the season progresses.

TOP LEFT Drystone walls provide plenty of crevices for invertebrates to shelter in, although plant-gobbling snails also like these homes.
DESIGN BY CAROLIEN BARKMAN

TOP RIGHT Very small or oddly-shaped areas can often be planted up with alpines; *Sempervivum* species can even grow vertically.
DESIGN BY ALTON INFANT SCHOOL

ABOVE Nectar-rich English marigolds (*Calendula officinalis*) and chives (*Allium schoenoprasum*) self-sow in most gardens.
DESIGN BY MARNEY HALL

OPPOSITE A log storage shelter fitted with a small green roof planted with dwarf sedums creates habitats for a wide range of creatures.
DESIGNY BY KAZUYUKI ISHIHARA

CASE STUDY: Suburban wildlife retreat

Design by Carrie Preston

FAR LEFT At the rear of the garden is a space Carrie calls 'the bird forest', a miniature woodland of small-growing trees and large shrubs, such as *Viburnum opulus* and varieties of *Amelanchier* and *Sorbus*. The rest of the planting makes extensive use of plants that were already in the garden before the new design, plus a few native species.

TOP CENTRE A tiny pond features a miniature water lily; ivy creeping down the walls provides a wildlife link and access route.

TOP LEFT A 'nest' of willow branches woven around sturdy upright chestnut poles, in conjunction with the plants at its base, offers shelter for invertebrates.

BELOW CENTRE A living willow fence along one side of the garden provides privacy while also supporting a range of insect habitats.

BELOW LEFT Vines are great plants for small wildlife gardens, offering decorative foliage and attractive fruit, which both garden owners and wildlife can benefit from.

Garden designer, Carrie Preston, an American living and working in the Netherlands, designed this garden for Gerda Timmermans and Annelies Gielen. A keen nature photographer, Gerda is also partially disabled and uses a wheelchair, so as well as wanting to maximise the wildlife in the garden, she needs places to sit and wait for birds or insects to photograph.

Carrie has made the long thin garden feel wider by setting rectangular blocks of paving slabs at right angles to the sides of the garden. A raised bench, also made from paving slabs with bamboo and twigs pushed between them, doubles as a space for Gerda to sit and a habitat for hibernating insects, such as solitary bees, including species of bumblebee.

WILDLIFE FEATURES

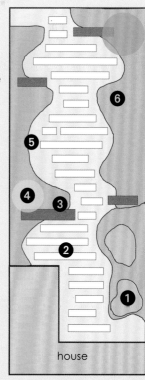

1. Small ponds for wildlife

2. Stepping stones in gravel, offering a permeable surface for water drainage

3. Paving slab seat/divider; invertebrates roost in the gaps

4. *Amelanchier lamarckii* offers food for wildlife

5. Stakes supporting woven willow – an invertebrate 'hotel' and hammock

6. A 'bird forest': layered shrub and perennial planting

GARDEN DIMENSIONS: approx 13m x 5.5m (43ft x 18ft)

house

7

Sustainable small spaces

Designs for compact eco-friendly gardens

The products and plants we include in our gardens all have an impact on the environment, but by choosing them carefully, we can make a positive contribution to the welfare of wildlife and minimise our carbon footprint.

Environmental factors to consider

Most people now want to be sustainable, especially in the garden where we are closest to nature. 'Sustainability' is best defined as an attempt to minimise the resources required to make or grow a product or plant, while also limiting harmful emissions. For gardeners, there are two factors that are particularly relevant.

1. Water management The worldwide supply of accessible, clean water is limited and, in the past, the gardening sector has been a shockingly wasteful user. Paradoxically, flooding, caused by too much water in the wrong place, is also on the increase. In urban areas, these problems are often linked, and the small garden owner can play an important role in making things better.

2. Hard material choices The construction industry, which includes garden landscaping, is the world's third largest contributor to carbon dioxide emissions, after energy and transport. Some professional designers and landscape contractors use large quantities of stone, brick or cement to create garden features, and very often the next owner of the property will rip these out and replace them with yet more unsustainable materials, exacerbating the problem.

So, how can we construct a garden that uses less water to maintain it, prevents water that falls on it from running into over-stretched sewers, and employs materials that tread lightly on the planet? There are a number of solutions that deliver benefits for all.

"Clean water is in short supply and the gardening sector has been a shockingly wasteful user."

LEFT Reusing materials, especially when locally sourced, increases a garden's sustainability.
DESIGN BY NIGEL DUNNETT & THE LANDSCAPE AGENCY

TOP RIGHT Green roofs reduce water runoff, minimising the impact on drainage systems.
DESIGN BY RITA HIGGINS & PAUL QUIRKE

BOTTOM RIGHT Stone setts allow water to drain through and soak into the ground.
DESIGN BY SUSAN SHARKEY

PREVIOUS PAGE A designer's garden makes clever use of recycled or reused materials.
DESIGN BY SPENCER VINER

LEFT You can create a green roof to absorb water runoff from a shed or house, if the construction is sturdy enough to take the load, or build a purpose-built structure such as this canopy.

TOP RIGHT Sloping roofs can be transformed into green ones with sufficient support for the substrate and plants, such as sedums.

CENTRE RIGHT Areas of planting at ground level can act as 'swales', which absorb excess water during storms, allowing it to soak away slowly and stay within the garden.
DESIGN BY MIKE HARVEY

BOTTOM RIGHT Growing drought-tolerant plants, such as alliums, grasses and lavender, is an easy way to reduce the volume of water needed for irrigation.
DESIGN BY ALEXANDRA NOBLE

Managing water in urban gardens

Towns and cities, with their hard, impermeable surfaces, tend to play havoc with the way water naturally cycles through the environment, but homeowners can perform a critical role in mitigating the problem. Some governments are now even offering incentives to create 'rain gardens', which alleviate flooding, while many have also introduced regulations that limit the creation of new hard surfaces, such as driveways and terracing.

Rain that lands on natural or semi-natural environments, such as forests or grassland, is largely absorbed into the ground, filtering down to join the underground reservoir known as the 'water table', and eventually seeping out into a stream or river. Some water stays on plants' foliage and quickly evaporates, but much is absorbed by their roots and eventually released through the leaves in a process called transpiration. Only in exceptional circumstances and in particular places will so much rain fall that natural processes cannot deal with it. In these instances, the excess water, or 'runoff', flows over the surface to form a flood.

Urban and other built-up areas disrupt this natural water cycle. There are few trees or other plants to absorb water in the ground, while the hard surfaces of buildings, roads and car parks dramatically increase runoff and the risk of flooding. Research also shows that where homeowners have paved over their front gardens, there has been a marked increase in flash floods caused by storm-water runoff.

Increasing water absorption

Private gardens often make up a substantial proportion of urban areas, so the actions of individual owners can have a great impact. One way of positively affecting your environment is to design a garden that does not impede the natural water cycle. Known as a 'rain garden', it will typically include some of the following elements:

- **Planted areas** that connect the soil directly to the water table, such as lawns, borders, trees and shrubs.
- **'Swales'** which are depressions designed to fill with water during storms and hold it temporarily until it can either soak into the ground or evaporate.
- **Porous hard surfaces** that allow water to soak away, or combine the functionality of a hard surface with planted areas.
- **Drains from buildings** that run into soakaways in the ground, rather than into a city sewer or other drainage system.
- **Water storage facilities** that direct rainwater falling on buildings into cisterns or tanks.
- **Green roofs** and other technologies, which trap water and hold it above ground until it evaporates or is taken up by the plants.

Planning and planting a mini rain garden

Limiting runoff from a small private garden has both a public benefit and a private one, as it reduces the likelihood of flooding in neighbouring properties, while also protecting your own. Increasingly, local governments are trying to persuade property owners with incentives to reduce runoff, so check what schemes and advice your authority is offering.

Most gardens, however small, contain some soil and plants, so rain will normally end up participating in a typical healthy water cycle (see p.141). However, if you experience localised flooding after a storm, you will need to make an area to hold the water, where it will cause minimal damage until it drains. In gardens where there is little soil and the ground is dominated by paving, water is more likely to accumulate and either flood or run off elsewhere. In these cases, building raised beds and filling them with imported soil will help absorb some of the rainwater. In other situations, flooding may be the result of compacted soil, perhaps left by builders after a new house construction, which is impeding drainage, and you will need to break through this impervious layer to remedy the problem.

BELOW *Iris ensata* and *Primula japonica* are two plants that thrive in damp soil but can also cope with occasional flooding, making them ideal for water detention basins. DESIGN BY LESLEY BREMNESS

BELOW *Phlox divaricata* and *Tiarella cordifolia* decorate the edges of this steel grid, which creates a raised walkway when the area below is filled with water after heavy rain. DESIGN BY NIGEL DUNNETT

Creating a swale

A key way to reduce runoff is to build a 'swale', which acts as a mini detention basin, holding water until it can either soak away or evaporate into the atmosphere – in other words, a temporary pond. In a small garden this need be no more than a depression with sloping sides, which will be the first place to fill with water when it rains and the last place to drain. This depression should also prevent your terrace, veg patch, or, worst of all, the house filling with water. An informal swale can be easily disguised in an area of planting, but in a patio garden, a more geometric shape that looks like a proper water feature may be best, with well-designed planting in and around it. Your plant choices will also determine the success of your swale, and they should survive occasional flooding but not require high water levels to flourish during average weather conditions. They need to have enough height and bulk to disguise the swale, too, or alternatively should be decorative and make an eye-catching feature. Planting options for swales are listed on p.144.

BELOW Gravel in a depression is designed to hold water after a storm, while the surrounding plants will not suffer during a deluge. This area could also be connected to a larger soakaway.
DESIGN BY ANDREW WILSON AND GAVIN McWILLIAM

BELOW This slate-filled trough is linked to the guttering on a roof and will hold water until it can drain away naturally. The planting and design also make an interesting garden feature.
DESIGN BY ADRIAN HALLAM, CHRIS ARROWSMITH & NIGEL DUNNETT

Planting choices for swales

These tough plants help to both disguise or augment a swale and provide ornamental interest for a more extensive rain garden. All will survive periods of flooding, as well as drier conditions.

SHRUBS

- *Amelanchier* species
- *Aronia* species
- *Cornus sanguinea*
- *Corylus avellana*
- *Fatsia japonica*
- *Hydrangea quercifolia*
- *Physocarpus opulifolius*
- *Salix*, smaller growing species
- *Viburnum*, European and North American species (pictured)

PERENNIALS

- *Aruncus dioicus*
- *Aster* species
- *Chelone* species
- *Echinacea pallida*
- *Eupatorium* species
- *Filipendula* species
- *Geranium* species
- *Iris sibirica* (pictured)
- *Monarda* species
- *Primula florindae*
- *Sanguisorba* species
- *Solidago* species
- *Trollius* species
- *Veronicastrum virginicum*

TOP LEFT Plants rooted in a depression in ordinary free-draining soil and covered with a stone mulch several centimetres thick maximise the volume of water that can be held there during a period of heavy rainfall.
DESIGN BY HADLOW COLLEGE

LEFT This ornamental swale is surrounded by a stone edging which gives it a more formal character. The *Iris pseudacorus* is normally grown as a pond-side marginal but does not need high water levels to thrive.
DESIGN BY ARNE MAYNARD

Installing a water butt

Collected rainwater is a valuable resource and can be used for watering the garden during dry weather. Once upon a time, houses often incorporated water-saving features, such as underground cisterns or wells, which trapped water that had drained off the roof. Retrofitting such systems is difficult, although not impossible, so most homeowners today are limited to using water butts. These are connected to the drainpipes on the house or garden outbuildings, which channel water into the butt rather than down the drain.

You will find a wide range of water butts of varying sizes, shapes and styles, as well as the connecting systems, at garden centres or on the internet. Choose from chic contemporary or barrel styles, or utilitarian plastic types if they will not be on view.

SINKING A SOAKAWAY

Deep pits filled with stone aggregate, soakaways are designed to hold water in the garden and then allow it to drain away slowly into the ground. They are usually connected to a drain, either from an area of hard standing, such as a patio or terrace, or to the drainpipes attached to the gutters on the house roof. You can integrate a soakaway into your garden design by covering it with soil and planting up the area with moisture lovers, or you can build a deck over it. A qualified builder or landscape company will be able to install one for you.

BELOW Soakaways are designed to hold and deal with substantial volumes of water. They can be made into a garden feature such as this one, or disguised with planting. DESIGN BY DARREN HAWKES

LEFT Water draining off a roof is directed into a water butt, disguised by timber cladding. To be useful, this would have to include a tap at a level where it can be accessed easily. DESIGN BY PHILIPPA PEARSON

Making hard surfaces porous

Hard surfaces, such as terraces, driveways, and concrete yards, prevent rain and surface water reaching the ground below and completing the natural water cycle, yet they are essential for those with small gardens, as the alternative is mud for much of the

"If you need to park cars on a driveway, you can choose from a range of porous materials."

year. Decking is a popular option, and if built with sustainably grown timber, it is a good one, allowing water to percolate through to the soil below, thereby reducing runoff. But unless blocked off, decking can also make an excellent rat habitat, which may be a problem in some urban areas. Its lifespan, even if well-maintained, will also never be as long as stone, brick, cement or paving, although a hard wood, such as ipe, will last many years. Brick, stone, and other hard surfaces are not only more durable than wood, their maintenance needs are generally lower too. The problem is, how can we ensure they are permeable?

Permeable paving solutions

Paving can be made porous but its ability to drain depends on how it is laid. Laying it on sand, without any cement to hold it in place, will allow water to run through the gaps and soak away underneath. Increasing the gap size between pavers and filling the spaces with gravel or other free-draining material will make paving even more porous. Try bricks or pavers, which offer more gaps per surface area than paving slabs and are easier to lay if you want an intricate design.

If you need to park cars on a driveway, you can now choose from a range of porous materials designed for this purpose, including those that combine load-bearing with the possibility of growing grass or other small creeping plants through them. Products include heavy-duty grass mesh, which integrates with a lawn and protects the turf when cars are parked on it, and specially designed grid stabilisers that help to keep gravel, which is completely porous, in place.

LEFT Gravel is porous, allowing water to drain through, but to function in a rain garden it needs to be laid on top of soil. DESIGN BY LUKE HEYDON

TOP RIGHT Paving separated by spaces that allow low, load-tolerant plants, such as chamomile, to grow through creates an unusual design effect.

CENTRE RIGHT Metal grids can be used for paving, paths or small bridges over water features or boggy ground that act as a reservoir after heavy rain. DESIGN BY KATE GOULD

BOTTOM RIGHT Low 'walk-on' plants can be laid in strips between bands of stone setts to form a permeable path. DESIGN BY CHARLOTTE ROWE

Introducing recycled and reused materials

Since the construction industry is such a major contributor to the carbon dioxide emissions responsible for climate change, it makes sense to take a critical look at the hard materials used in gardens and seek alternatives. Paving is probably the most commonly used material, followed by bricks, stones and cement used to build retaining walls, and wood for fencing, screens and garden furniture. However, all construction materials cannot be categorised uniformly as 'good' or 'bad' and their eco-friendly credentials depend on a number of factors.

Assessing energy consumption

In most cases, the less a material has to be processed, the more sustainable it is. Think about the difference between a brick and a stone, both produced relatively close to where you live. The stone exists already, but the brick has to be baked from clay, so the brick has higher embodied energy, making it less sustainable. But both can be reused, and indeed secondhand bricks are very attractive building materials, lending a patina of age that can otherwise take decades to achieve. Old bricks can also be processed and turned into a product sold as 'crushed brick', which is a useful alternative to gravel, or you can use it as substrate for green roofs. But to make bricks into crushed bricks requires energy, too, and so this product will have higher embodied energy than gravel.

Choosing a style for small gardens

'Recycled' still has echoes of a particular style associated with early green activists and a bohemian way of making and doing things. It is a look that appeals to some, but not everyone wants their garden to *appear* recycled. Today there is greater choice, with an increasing number of products made from recycled materials that look as clean and modern as any other product, the recycling having been concealed in the manufacturing process.

Those who have consciously created a traditional recycled style are probably using salvaged rather than recycled materials. 'Salvage style' has a charm of its own, derived from the knowledge that what is being used had a previous life, which can evoke surprise when it has a different purpose in the garden. The previous life of salvaged goods forms part of their allure and is particularly important to those who are trying to use as much as possible from their site. Salvage style revels in its inventiveness, reminding onlookers of the skill of its creator. Pieces or constructions often carry with them stories of the architectural salvage yard, skip or roadside they were found in or on and tend to celebrate the urban, or even the industrial.

BELOW Old timbers may be uneven but this is part of their charm, as well as the silvery patina many develop.
DESIGN BY EMIEL VERSLUIS

RIGHT Decking allows the designer more creative flexibility; here re-used timbers are cantilevered over a canal at the end of a small garden in the Netherlands.
DESIGN BY MENEER VERMEER TUINEN

Salvaged hard landscaping materials

Timber is probably the easiest material to reuse without its antecedents being too obvious. Fences, furniture, sheds, and retaining walls can all incorporate timber that has had a previous life. Decking and walkways can also be made from salvaged wood, but it will need to be treated with preservative if it is to be in contact with damp ground. Also remember that most timber products with industrial origins, such as pallets, are made from poor quality softwood and will quickly decay.

Secondhand paving or kerb stones are particularly useful materials, and are sometimes available in large quantities. These can often be reused in a way that makes it almost impossible to guess that they are not new. Damaged secondhand bricks that are not suitable for a wall could also find another life as pavers, while broken slabs can be arranged to make 'crazy paving',

a retro style that has been around since the 1960s. Given the abundance of re-usable concrete and brick in our towns and cities, there is ample scope for many creative endeavours in the garden. There is even a new name for this material – urbanite.

Recycled materials for modern gardens

Truly recycled materials generally try to disguise their origin. An increasing number of attractive products for construction and paving are actually made from composites of recycled hardcore, while plastics are being recycled into new products too; again, most betray few signs of their origins and make decorative additions to small contemporary designs. Particularly robust is the dense plastic composite material, now available for decking, raised beds, benches and seats, which resembles the wood used for railway sleepers.

ALTERNATIVES TO CONCRETE

The manufacture of cement, which is the main material in concrete, contributes significantly to global carbon dioxide emissions. Although it has many advantages in the garden, there are often alternatives, particularly for landscaping. Soil, with a percentage of clay, can be made into cob, a traditional building material ideal for small garden structures and clay ovens. Soil can also be used to make rammed earth walls. Although many of these 'ecological' construction techniques use bulky materials, they are usually sourced locally, minimising transport costs, and most require little energy to produce.

The use of reinforced concrete is common in the construction of retaining walls. In hilly areas, small garden owners often need walls to create level terraces that make their space usable, or to stop either their neighbours' garden sliding down onto theirs or their plot sliding into the neighbours'. Among the best alternatives to concrete for these sturdy structures are gabions. Heavy-duty wire boxes, gabions can be filled with loose stones or rubble, which require no cement. They can also be used to build low garden walls or screens (pictured below), supports for benches, and for the foundations of garden buildings.

OPPOSITE LEFT Recycled heavy timbers cut to size and used as stepping stones in a shingle base allow maximum permeability, but shingle will only have low 'transport miles' if the garden is close to the coast.
DESIGN BY CHRIS O'DONOGHUE

OPPOSITE RIGHT This new-style crazy paving, with plenty of grit-filled space between the slabs, allows water to drain and ground-hugging plants, such as sedums and thymes, to thrive. These little plants also tolerate being walked on occasionally.
DESIGN BY FLORIS STEYAERT

BELOW AND BELOW LEFT Gabions are more eco-friendly than many hard landscaping features and can be taken apart and reused. They also create spaces for invertebrates, and even provide sites for nectar-rich plants and nesting birds.
DESIGN BY YVONNE MATHEWS (BELOW LEFT)

8

Containers for small plots

Creative displays for containers

Growing plants in pots is a great way of injecting more colour and interest into a small garden, but for the most effective displays, ensure you choose suitable plants and be prepared to feed and water them regularly.

Flexible arrangements

Growing plants in containers is fun, but it can also be hard work, since pots are vulnerable to drying out. It's like high-wire gardening – you can create a great spectacle, it's immensely rewarding, but it can also be potentially disastrous if things go wrong.

Let's start with the fun part. Containers offer flexibility because they can be easily moved around, unless, of course, they are so large and heavy or an integral part of the garden design that they have to stay put. And while plants in the ground should remain in situ for at least one growing season, those in pots can be swapped so that only the best performers are on show. You can also chop and change the arrangement of your pots, perhaps to create a more artistic display or for functional reasons, such as making way for a dinner party.

You are free to experiment when growing plants in containers. Some designers use pots to assess the success of various plant combinations, moving them around until they find a place they are happy with, before planting out permanently. You can do the same: try something new, change it immediately if it does not work, or give it a few weeks and then alter the arrangement if necessary. Plants often go through good phases and bad phases, too, and it is nice to be able to put those that are looking their best in pride of place, and shuffle those that are past it, but still have potential, into positions where they are less visible.

LEFT Pink flowers are set off by blue raised beds on this rooftop garden. Deep blue pots continue the colour theme, while terracotta and recycled vessels add a personal touch. DESIGN BY WILLY MEIJER & HANS ROSIER

TOP RIGHT Recycled food cans are used here as planters, adding a quirky touch to the shelves in this modern garden. DESIGN BY NADA HABET

CENTRE RIGHT Unattractive or functional pots can be hidden in baskets and other containers which, by themselves, would be quite impractical for holding soil and plants.

BOTTOM RIGHT Repeated pots of the same design and colour have great impact, and help to focus attention on the plants while drawing the eye through the garden. DESIGN BY SPECIAL TREES

PREVIOUS PAGE The containers in this tiny garden offer the flexibility to swap plants, so that only those at their peak are on show. DESIGN BY DICK HUIGENS/GARDENS OF APPELTERN

Choosing containers

Many gardeners use containers for seasonal plants, such as bulbs in spring, colourful bedding in summer, and grasses or foliage plants through autumn and winter. This method of growing plants allows you to ring the changes year on year, trying out different combinations, alternative colour themes and a range of plant varieties. The type of container you choose is important too, and one of the really fun aspects of working with pots is making attractive, quirky, or even provocative matches between the vessel and the plants growing in it.

Artistically minded gardeners may place more emphasis on the containers they choose, while plant-lovers often treat their pots in a totally functional way. For them, the container is a means to an end, offering a way of creating a garden where there is no soil, for example, or including tender plants that need to come inside for winter protection, or simply producing 'virtual borders' where the components can be moved around. For these gardeners, containers need to be almost invisible, allowing the plants to shine without distraction. Others may want to use their pots to create a particular design, either combining similar types for a complementary look or an assortment of styles that heighten the drama and creative tension.

Material options

The wide array of containers on the market offers something for every garden size and style. Particularly useful are those made from modern materials, such as glass fibre, resin, plastic, or wood composite, which imitate natural materials that are either very heavy or expensive. Terracotta, stone and lead imitations of historic models make life much easier and cheaper for those who want to evoke a classical look in their garden or on their terrace. They are also lighter and therefore safer if you are designing displays for a balcony or roof garden. New materials have increased

the range of styles on offer, too, with brightly coloured pots and large and unusual contemporary designs widely available at affordable prices.

The rustic look, created with containers made from wood and other natural materials, is rarely out of fashion. Although these containers very often lack durability, most can go on the compost heap when they're past their prime and do not create a disposal problem. Many rustic materials are useful as skins or screens for more durable pots; for example, basket-like structures made from woven willow can be used to conceal unattractive or purely functional plastic pots, and the life of the willow will also be prolonged because it is not in contact with wet compost.

Vintage materials provide plenty of scope for creative gardeners, and if sourced well, they can also offer a major cost advantage, particularly if you are looking for large structures. All sorts of products can be reused as plant containers: old metal buckets, drainage pipes, bulk food containers, oil cans – the options are endless. Just remember to drill drainage holes in the bottom of your vessels to ensure your plants don't drown, and check that they were not used to hold harmful chemicals in a previous life.

OPPOSITE LEFT A saucepan is home to a tomato plant, which will need to be a 'bush' variety to thrive in this tight space.

OPPOSITE RIGHT A deep copper trough offers enough root room for some permanent plants, such as ivy and a sedge. Other temporary seasonal elements, such as campanulas, have also been included.
DESIGN BY NEIL GOLDSMITH & SABINA EDWARDS

BELOW LEFT Containers can be used to mix and match edible crops, such as the beetroots and chives here. Violas add a little flower colour and are a good choice for a productive display, since both the blooms and leaves are edible too.
DESIGN BY LAURIE CHETWOOD & PATRICK COLLINS

BELOW RIGHT The flowering bulb, *Anemone blanda,* in this basket will be succeeded by forget-me-nots (*Myosotis sylvatica*) that will continue the display into early summer. After flowering the anemones can be planted in the garden, ready to flower again next year.

Shaping up

While containers come in all shapes and sizes, some are more suitable for plants than others. Remember that the larger the pot, the more compost and moisture it will hold, and therefore the less frequently you will have to water it. Traditional pots, which are wider at the top than the bottom, are perfect for plants, since they provide plenty of space for the roots to grow, and you can remove them easily when you want to repot them. Taller pots, which offer even more root room, are vital for some plants and the best choice for many shrubs and climbers, such as roses and clematis.

Plants are more difficult to remove from straight-sided containers, although if you are only growing annuals this is not a big issue. Large plant containers, often referred to as 'planters', are nearly always straight-sided but because of their size they tend to be left in place and you can remove plants from them by digging them out.

Some pots are only suitable for specific types of plant, and if you choose them, make your selections carefully. Wall pots with very wide semi-circular tops and narrow bottoms dry out rapidly and are unsuitable for most plants apart from succulents, unless you can water daily in warm or dry weather. Pots with an incurved top, such as small-necked urns, are a nightmare if you want to remove established perennial plants without damaging either plants or pot – even dead annuals can be difficult to extract. If you like this style, avoid these problems by planting up a small plastic pot that fits snugly into the neck of the urn.

PLANTING IN SHALLOW CONTAINERS

Shallow containers that are less than 20cm (8in) in height provide a restricted area for rooting and are prone to drying out. They are really only suitable for small plants, but can make decorative additions to the garden if they are watered frequently.

Very shallow containers, with a depth of less than 10cm (4in), have traditionally been used for growing diminutive alpine plants. Many species, such as varieties of dwarf *Dianthus*, will grow well, but most flower in spring. Choose those with decorative evergreen foliage, including houseleeks (*Sempervivum*), sedums and *Phlox*, to ensure a longer season of interest.

PLANT OPTIONS

- *Antennaria dioica*
- *Campanula* – dwarf forms, e.g. *C. cochlearifolia*
- *Delosperma* species
- *Phlox subulata*
- *Rhodiola* species
- *Scleranthus* species
- *Sedum* – alpine species
- *Sempervivum* species (pictured)
- *Veronica prostrata*

RIGHT Violas are ideal for container growing, as they are hardy, flower in cold weather, and are cheap to buy. Longevity varies, but many will last a year.

BELOW Lantanas are tropical plants that flower when little more than rooted cuttings. They will provide several months of summer colour, often until the first frosts.

OPPOSITE Shelving enables the gardener to swap plants around so they can be appreciated when at their best. These tulips and other spring bulbs will be replaced with summer bedding after the frosts.
DESIGN BY JAN TALSMA & FOKKE BLOEMSMA

MASTERCLASS
TOP CONTAINER DESIGN TIPS

It is tempting to combine perennials and shrubs with annuals in larger containers, but the success of the grouping depends very much on the extent of the perennial or shrub's root system. The easiest option is to play it safe and keep long-lived plants in large, separate pots, which can remain in the same place year after year. This permanent element will provide long-term structure and foliage interest, and you can then add to the display with annuals in smaller containers, which can be moved around as their level of interest increases or decreases. A good approach for beginners is to experiment with some cheap or fast-growing shrubs and perennials and build up experience of what succeeds best in a pot.

Bulbs combine more easily with other long-term plants, as many are in growth in spring before the majority of perennials and shrubs; small daffodils, crocuses and snowdrops are the most reliable for year-on-year performance.

The following guidelines will help you to achieve the best results, either by combining separate plants in their own pots, or bringing together a range in large containers. Choose specific plants from the recommendations on p.158 and p.166.

Tallest at the back, shortest at the front
This is a basic principle for traditional border plantings and a good starting point for containers too. In small spaces, it is a sensible approach, and ensures that all plants can be seen, and the shorter forms hide the sometimes less attractive lower stems of taller ones. Where there is no 'front' or 'back', then 'tallest in the middle' applies.

Rely on mass
Plants fall easily into one of three basic categories: tall and upright, medium-sized mass, and small and spreading. If most of the plants you use fall into the middle category, they will give your container combinations weight and a good physical presence, and you will always have something to look at, even when the plants are not in flower.

Limit the drama
There are certain plants that draw attention to themselves, most notably those with height, dramatic or large leaves, or far-flung but airy stems. These are essential for drama and interest but are easily overdone. If placed close together, they can physically get in each other's way too, so check that their stems and leaves have sufficient space.

LEFT Functional, even downright ugly, plastic containers can always be hidden inside others, such as these rustic wicker baskets and ceramic pots.
DESIGN BY TON VISSERS/ GARDENS OF APPELTERN

Pack them in

Seasonal plantings, such as annuals, look best if they are exuberant and fulsome, and, besides, you probably want to use them to maximise their impact. Closely-packed annuals in containers will need regular watering and feeding, but they will grow amicably together and produce flowers all summer if the faded blooms are removed.

Less is more

Some people like the 'sweet-box' approach, combining lots of colours and plant varieties, but paring down the number of shapes, shades and species creates a more sophisticated look, ideal for a contemporary display. Extend this elegance to the containers, too, and choose those with simple graphic shapes made from good quality materials.

Remember the little ones

Small spreading plants are always useful for filling gaps and creating interest right down to the bottom or edge of your container display. Just remember that some plants, including alpines and the succulents shown here, also need full sun, so pot them up separately and ensure they are not overshadowed by the larger specimens in your scheme.

Container care

Containers can provide a colourful addition to your small garden, but remember that plants in pots need constant care. As they are not in contact with the soil, their roots cannot extend outwards and reach down to draw on the moisture reserves in the ground. Instead, they are totally dependent on rainfall and on you for their water supplies. Likewise, nutrient levels can quickly become depleted in pots, and containerised plants will need feeding regularly.

Plants in pots are also far more vulnerable to temperature extremes: in winter the compost will freeze more quickly and more thoroughly than the soil in the ground, and it will also heat up and dry out rapidly during the summer months. But despite the disadvantages, there are many benefits to growing plants in containers from a horticultural point of view. Here are a few reasons to give it a go:

> **"Plants in pots are totally dependent on rainfall and on you for their water supplies, and they need feeding regularly."**

- **Plants can be moved** around to suit their needs. Spring-flowering shade-lovers can be given the pride of place when they are performing and then shuffled off into a quiet spot during the warm summer months, while tall pots filled with compact summer annuals can be inserted into the middle of a border to fill seasonal gaps.
- **Tender, even sub-tropical, plants** can be placed outside for the summer, where they are more likely to stay healthy and pest free. They can then be enjoyed as part of the garden design, before being moved back indoors for winter.
- **Different soil conditions** can be provided for, allowing plant combinations that would be impossible in the garden. For example, you can place pots of lime-lovers, such as *Dianthus* (pinks) alongside lime-haters, such as *Skimmia* and *Rhododendron* species, or bog plants next to dry habitat species.

TOP LEFT Busy Lizzies – hybrids of *Impatiens* – have long been popular as summer container plants, particularly for shady areas of the garden.
DESIGN BY DE LIMIETEN

CENTRE LEFT A variegated hosta is placed in a pot to echo the yellow of

a flowering *Potentilla fruticosa* behind.
DESIGN BY GEOFFREY WHITEN

BOTTOM LEFT *Pieris japonica* 'Katsura' is grown here as a container plant. A large shrub for acid soils, it will only be happy in a pot for a short while and will then need a permanent home.

Which compost where?

The material used for growing plants is, somewhat confusingly, called 'compost' – 'substrate' is the more technical term and causes less confusion with the substance you remove from a compost heap. The nature of the substrate is crucial, and determines a plant's ability to access moisture and nutrients. Your choice depends on whether you are growing short-lived annual plants, or perennials or shrubs that will be in their containers for a few years. The longer the plant is going to be in its pot, the more care you need to take in choosing a compost and the more you should be prepared to spend. Potting composts can be made from many materials, but those listed in the box below are the most commonly used for containers.

CONTAINER COMPOST CHOICES

- **Soil-based potting composts**
  Many experts say that these composts, made from sterilised loam, are the best of all, and they are a good choice for long-term plantings of shrubs, climbers, and perennials. However, they are relatively expensive and heavy, and their weight can be a real problem (and a health issue) if pots are moved around regularly. But weight can be an advantage in windy locations or where tall or top-heavy plants are being grown; in such situations, soil-based composts, possibly with grit added for even more stability, are a good idea.

- **Peat-free composts**
  These are usually made from composted plant material. They are often cheap and light, but vary in quality. Some may leave plants short of nutrients much more quickly than composts comprised of other materials. However, they are good choice for short-lived plantings, such as summer bedding, but are liable to break down over time and are therefore less suitable for shrubs or perennials that will be in their pots for many years.

- **Peat-based composts**
  For decades, these dominated the market until concerns were raised over their environmental impact. This criticism is not always justified; peat extraction can, in fact, be a sustainable process. The great advantage of peat is its combination of lightness and longevity, so if you have long-term plants, it is worth considering this type of compost. Gardeners concerned about the environmental impact of peat extraction may wish to do their own research.

- **Home-produced composts**
  You can make your own planting material from a mixture of garden soil and garden compost, but it is rarely as effective as proprietary bought types. This is because homemade compost tends to break down quickly and it is often full of weed seeds and may also harbour pests and diseases.

- **Green roof substrates**
  Specialist lightweight products, these substrates have been developed for green roofs. They have a low organic content, which means they do not break down quickly, and are useful for long-term plantings. They are now widely available and ideal for potted plants of any sort.

Watering techniques

The number one factor affecting the success or failure of plants in pots is watering. Many plants are seriously damaged if the compost dries out, either through failure to water on a very hot day, or, more gradually, by chronic underwatering over many months. As anyone who has house plants will know, the opposite problem – overwatering – can be equally damaging. Waterlogging is often caused by placing containers on saucers filled with water, or by blocked drainage holes. The roots then die off due to lack of oxygen and become infected by fungal and bacterial pathogens, which go on to attack the healthy roots, killing the plant.

Most plants in containers need good drainage to prevent waterlogging – the only exceptions are bog plants. Check that any pots you buy have drainage holes in the base; ideally, these need to be large enough to ensure they do not to get blocked and that water drains through easily. Standing pots on 'feet', which raise the base off the ground, also helps to prevent blockages. It is widely believed that drainage is improved by placing stones or pieces of broken terracotta over the drainage holes, but this is a myth and they are not necessary.

You can choose an automatic water system (see below) or, if you have just a few containers and sufficient time, you can simply water by hand using a can or hose. When watering, ensure you aim at the compost, rather than spraying it over the leaves and flowers, as the water may simply run off them and over the edge of the pot, thereby missing its target.

WATERING SYSTEMS

A wide range of irrigation systems have been developed to help gardeners water their pots. Some operate from outdoor taps, others from containers of stored water. The latter can be used for captured rainwater, offering a good sustainable solution, although you need space for the water storage facilities and some are not very attractive and best hidden between pots.

Automatic watering systems can be very effective, and comprise small drippers attached to pipes that connect to your outside tap. A timer fixed to the tap will ensure your pots are watered daily and you can set it to operate early

in the morning or in the evening when evaporation rates are lowest. The water also trickles directly into the compost, thereby reducing wastage.

Consider the options carefully, perhaps by going to a garden show where mock-ups are on display.

LEFT When plants, such as strawberries, are actively growing, and the compost is free-draining, it is almost impossible to overwater, but take care as growth slows down, when roots can drown.

Feeding plants in containers

If they are not fed well, plants in containers are likely to starve, resulting in poor growth and yellow or discoloured foliage. However, you do not necessarily want them to perform *too* well, as they may quickly outgrow their pot; the dwarfing effect of growing large plants, particularly woody species, in pots can be a real advantage – think of Chinese and Japanese bonsai.

Feeding the right amount keeps plants healthy, growing well and, crucially, flowering profusely. Any compost sold in a bag contains nutrients, but these only keep plants going for a limited period, which is usually stated on the packaging. Some perennials and shrubs can be kept in pots for years without feeding, but they are not typical; most need an application of fertiliser at least once a year, and those that flower continuously, like summer bedding, require a constant supply of nutrients.

Plant nutrition is a complex business, but most gardeners only need to know one bit of chemistry, one bit of methodology, and one bit of maths (see box, right). Whether a fertiliser is 'organic' or not is, scientifically speaking, irrelevant to plants' health.

When using any fertiliser, follow the dosage guidelines on the packaging: overfeeding can be as detrimental as giving too little.

ABOVE LEFT Fertiliser dissolved in water is the most common method of feeding plants; applying it regularly is vital.

LEFT A slow-release fertiliser pellet is an easy way to provide your plants with a long-term supply of food.

FERTILISERS FOR POTTED PLANTS

- **Liquid fertilisers** You can buy bottles of liquid plant food or dry chemical powders, which need to be diluted with water. Either way, you should apply these fertilisers throughout the growing season, usually weekly. They can be applied when watering, and are most appropriate for annuals, and fruit and vegetable plants.

- **Slow-release fertilisers** If you do not have time to feed your plants every week, choose a slow-release fertiliser. These comprise small pellets or granules, which are mixed with the compost at the beginning of the growing season, or when plants start to show signs of hunger. The nutrients are released slowly over many months and one application is usually sufficient for the year. Also, the warmer it is, the quicker they release their nutrients. Application rates are usually given on the pack, often as grammes per litre of compost (1 litre = 1,000 cubic centimetres). To simplify things, weigh out a teaspoon of granules using digital kitchen scales, and note it down. Working out volume is easy arithmetic for square containers (width x length x height) but for circular ones, we need this formula: $\pi \times r^2 \times h$, where $\pi = 3.14$ (pi), r^2 = the radius of the pot multiplied by itself, and h = the height of the pot. Simple! Write down how many teaspoons you require for each of your pot sizes and keep the information for next year.

- **High-potash fertilisers** Most plant foods are general fertilisers, and include a balance of the various nutrients plants need. However, one nutrient, potash, helps to encourage flowering and fruiting (and strong growth for resisting winter cold). Any product branded a 'tomato fertiliser' is the best source of potash, along with other nutrients; even if you are not growing tomatoes, it is good stuff for *Impatiens*, petunias, dahlias (right), pelargoniums and other bedding.

Choosing plants for pots in small gardens

You can select almost any annual plant for a container; they nearly always do well in confined spaces since they have shallow roots. Many perennials also grow happily in pots, although drought-tolerant types will be easiest to care for. Trees and shrubs obviously need large containers, but choose your species carefully, as their root systems vary enormously – a factor that can determine their success in a pot but which cannot often be discerned just by looking at them. Shallow-rooted types will thrive better than deep-rooted species.

Perennials for containers

Providing long-term colour and texture, many perennials are perfect for pots, but most will need to be lifted and divided after a few years.

- Achillea species
- Agapanthus (pictured below left)
- Agastache species
- Alchemilla mollis
- Astilbe species
- Calamintha species
- Centranthus ruber
- Convallaria majalis
- Dianthus species
- Echinacea species
- Epimedium species
- Geranium species
- Helleborus x hybridus
- Heuchera species
- Hosta species (pictured above left)
- Limonium platyphyllum
- Nepeta species
- Osteospermum species
- Penstemon species
- Primula species
- Salvia species
- Saxifraga species
- Sedum species
- Sisyrinchium species
- Veronica species

See also p.158

Woody plants for containers

Those with an asterisk* are shallow-rooted and flourish in containers but have a zero tolerance of drying out and prefer a cool situation.

TREES AND SHRUBS FOR LARGE POTS

- Acer palmatum (smaller forms) *
- Albizia julibrissin
- Betula nana
- Buxus sempervirens
- Camellia species * (pictured top left)
- Convolvulus cneorum
- Cordyline australis
- Corokia cotoneaster
- Cytisus species
- Daphne species
- Erica species *
- Eucalyptus species
- Euonymus fortunei and E. japonicus
- Ficus carica (see right)
- Fuchsia species (pictured centre left)
- Hebe species
- Hydrangea species
- Ilex species
- Laurus nobilis
- Myrtus communis
- Pittosporum species
- Rhododendron species *
- Rosmarinus officinalis
- Ruta graveolens
- Skimmia species
- Syringa meyeri
- Viburnum – spring-flowering varieties
- Yucca species

CLIMBERS FOR POTS

- Clematis - small types (pictured bottom left)
- Hedera species
- Jasminum species
- Trachelospermum jasminoides

LEFT These fig trees in deep containers are vigorous plants and will need pruning with time. There is plenty of space below them for other plants, but they will increasingly have to compete with the figs for nutrients, so feeding will be very important to sustain their health.
DESIGN BY ERWIN STAM

CASE STUDY: Potted front garden

Design by David Cund and Sally Golding

FAR LEFT Using ideas employed for flower show displays, plants are positioned to create a fulsome spectacle that also allows sufficient light to reach each plant.

TOP LEFT AND RIGHT Many cannas are grown for their variegated leaves, as well as for the flowers, which double their impact in tight spaces. The dark-leaved annual grass in front is *Setaria italica* 'Red Jewel'.

BELOW LEFT The annual castor oil plant (*Ricinus communis*) sports bold bronze leaves.

BELOW RIGHT *Carex oshimensis* 'Evergold', a hardy sedge, flourishes year after year in a recycled tin.

Sally Golding and David Cund have only the tiniest space at the front of their terraced house, but with a few containers they have managed to put together a vibrant planting combination. At first sight it actually looks like a garden, since many of the pots are not visible, but the plants are arranged in a way that would not be possible if they were in the ground. Creating what is essentially a stage set for their plants, some are in galvanised containers, others in large pots, while a number are standing on bricks to ensure each performer can be seen from the front.

In the winter, foliage sustains the interest, but summer sees the addition of a range of brightly-coloured flowers and leaves, including canna lilies, dahlias, and rudbeckias. Many are tender, and David overwinters these in his friend's old industrial greenhouse, which he also uses in spring to start off seedlings, such as those of the bronze-leaved *Ricinus communis*.

PLANTS USED

1. *Musa basjoo*
2. *Macleaya cordata*, with *Canna* and *Setaria* in front
3. *Ricinus communis*
4. *Rudbeckia* cultivar
5. *Heuchera villosa* 'Palace Purple'
6. *Pelargonium crispum*
7. *Carex siderosticha* 'Variegata'
8. *Carex oshimensis* 'Evergold'
9. *Nephrolepis exaltata*

GARDEN DIMENSIONS: approx 3m x 1.5m (10 x 5ft)

Making space for food

Creating a tiny fruit and vegetable plot

A garden with limited space should not deter you from growing at least some of your fruit and vegetables. Pack in the foods that you most enjoy and savour the intense flavours and freshness of homegrown produce.

Growing your own

There is something deeply emotionally satisfying about growing your own food. Even if you have space for just a small quantity of produce, its freshness, and knowledge of where it is from and what went into growing it, are hugely important. And for children, growing their own food often lays the foundations for a lifelong love of gardening.

Space is likely to be a major constraint on any attempts at even partial self-sufficiency in a small garden, and unless you are prepared to turn over every square centimetre to growing your own food, you are unlikely to produce more than a handful of crops. This makes the decision about what to grow even more important. Some people are guided by the fruits and vegetables that are not easily available to buy in the shops, or you can choose crops that you, or the family member who cooks, value for their freshness.

Also look for ways of cramming in more productivity. Tree fruits, such as apples, pears and cherries, can provide a substantial crop on a relatively small footprint, although they may cast shade over other areas of the garden. Small patches of veg can be shoehorned into ornamental borders too. Climbing or tall vegetable plants, such as runner beans and tomatoes, take up little space and can add to the decorative value of the garden when flowering and fruiting, while pots of herbs and salad crops will make leafy displays on a terrace.

LEFT This inventive design makes the most of areas with no true soil, with a pot of 'Ragged Jack' kale and nasturtiums nestling between productive raised beds. DESIGN BY BUNNY GUINNESS

TOP RIGHT Check that you have sufficient space between your crops to sow and harvest them. Narrow pathways will prevent you standing on the soil and compacting it.

CENTRE RIGHT Growing food just outside your back door allows children to get

involved at their own pace. Giving them a small patch of their own to cultivate will also encourage them and heighten their interest.

BOTTOM RIGHT Swiss chard is one of the best vegetables for a small garden, as it crops over a very long season, looks good, and does not need full sunlight to thrive.

PREVIOUS PAGE Tiered raised beds offer a neat way of getting as much vegetable growing space as possible into a tight spot. DESIGN BY PAUL STONE

MASTERCLASS
TYPES OF VEGETABLE

Vegetables tend to fall into a number of slightly overlapping categories. Typically, most gardeners with small plots will concentrate on quick and easy types that grow and can be harvested in a matter of months. Many can be grown easily in large pots or raised beds, but remember that they will need watering and feeding regularly to produce a good harvest.

> "Short-lifespan crops include a number of Asian varieties that are not often available to buy or carry a high quota of air miles."

❶ Short-lifespan crops

These can be harvested a few weeks to three months after sowing and are perhaps the best crops to grow in a small garden. There are many varieties to choose from, including a number from Asia that are not often available to buy or carry a high quota of air miles. For all the crops here, absolute freshness is also important, and those grown in your garden will always beat produce from any other source. Crops include:

- Salad leaf crops: lettuce (pictured), radish, rocket, spring onion
- Stir-fry greens: mostly oriental, such as mizuna, pak choi, komatsuna, kai-lan, and bomdong, but also spinach, raab (a kind of high-speed broccoli), callaloo (*Amaranthus* species), kale (eaten as baby kale) and peas grown for their shoots
- Annual, biennial or tender herbs: coriander, basil, and dill

❷ Medium-lifespan crops

Spending three to six months in the ground, these crops include some root and stem vegetables, broccoli, peas, and beans. The roots and kohlrabi are often eaten when relatively young, but can be left in the ground to be harvested during the winter. Florence fennel should be eaten as soon as it is ready, since it flowers (or 'bolts') very quickly. Peas and beans tend to be large and need canes or sticks to climb up, but the so-called 'dwarf' French beans are ideal for small gardens, while runner beans have such pretty flowers that they can double as ornamentals. Crops include:

- Faster-growing root vegetables: beetroot, carrot, turnip, winter radish and Asian mooli radish
- Some broccoli and calabrese varieties
- Kohlrabi and Florence fennel
- Peas and beans (French beans – pictured)

❸ Longer-term crops

These crops take a whole growing season to mature or are left in the ground to be eaten over winter, or the following spring. Most take up too much space for too long to bother with in small gardens. Winter brassicas, such as cabbages and Brussels sprouts, are also famously unattractive, and they build up soil diseases, which means they should not be grown in the same place for more than one year in every three. Swiss chard, however, is an exception: its compact size, relative shade tolerance and potential to crop for nearly 12 months, makes it one of the best vegetables for the small garden. Crops include:

- Brassicas: broccoli, Brussels sprouts, cabbage, cauliflower, kale
- Celery and celeriac
- Garlic, leeks, onions
- Leaf beets, such as Swiss chard (pictured)
- Parsnips
- Potatoes ('early' varieties may be in the ground for only a few months)

❹ Half-hardy crops

Although these crops need to be sown inside (in climates with spring frosts) and die after the first autumn frost, they are popular, as they produce quick results, offer a plethora of varieties, and often flourish in sheltered town gardens. Furthermore, nothing beats a freshly picked tomato. Unless bought as young plants, raising them from seed requires commitment, as seedlings need good light and warmth for a month prior to planting them out. Plants also need sun and some heat for the fruits to ripen. Crops include:

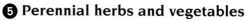

- Tomatoes (pictured)
- Aubergines
- Capsicum and chilli peppers
- Cucumbers
- Courgettes and marrows
- Pumpkins and squashes
- Sweet corn

❺ Perennial herbs and vegetables

Of the vegetables in this group, only the globe artichoke is known as a conventional vegetable, its wonderful silver foliage doubling up as an ornamental. Others are used in East Asian cuisines, and some people are also now growing perennial forage crops, such as wild garlics, as garden plants. A huge advantage of growing perennial vegetables is that they require far less work than annuals and biennials, and some, such as the herbs, are also easy to integrate into ornamental borders, especially in a sunny garden. Crops include:

- Perennial/shrubby herbs: sage, thyme, oregano, rosemary
- Globe artichokes (pictured)
- Edible ornamentals, e.g. Hemerocallis (daylily), hostas, knotweeds
- Forage crops, e.g. wild garlics

MASTERCLASS
TYPES OF FRUIT

Fruit-bearing plants are more permanent than most vegetables, and because they also tend to be larger, they require more spatial planning. For our ancestors, making a garden, even a small one, without tree or bush fruits would have been almost inconceivable, and many gardeners today are realising the benefits of including them. Most bushes and trees are relatively easy to grow, although they require regular pruning.

> "For our ancestors, making a garden without including tree or bush fruits would have been almost inconceivable."

❶ Tree fruit

When considering fruit trees for a small garden, factor in the space they will take up, and ensure you have the time to prune them each year. As flowering plants, they are very attractive, earning their keep twice over. Some fruit trees, notably apples and cherries, include small-growing varieties, which are a real boon to gardeners with limited space. The key to choosing trees is the 'rootstock'. Trees are usually grafted, whereby two different varieties are joined together at the base, with the rootstock controlling the rate of growth and ultimate size. Apples grafted on an M27 rootstock reach just 1.2m (4ft) high, while dwarf varieties on an M9 rootstock will grow to about 2.4m (7ft 10in). Some nurseries even sell 'step-over' apples, which are knee-height and trained horizontally. Cherries are limited to 3m (9ft 10in) when grown on a Gisella 5 rootstock, but other tree fruits are not grown on such dwarfing rootstocks, although small varieties may be available.

Recommended trees, from the smallest varieties at the top, include:

- Apples (pictured top)
- Pears
- Cherries (pictured bottom)
- Apricots
- Plums and damsons

❷ Patio fruit trees, cordons, and espaliers

Specially bred for growing in containers or very small spaces, 'patio' fruit trees are an option for those with just a courtyard or terrace. However, the fruit production of these tiny trees is limited, and they are perhaps a bit of a gimmick. Cordons, on the other hand, are a more traditional way of managing apples and pears, and they are genuinely productive – trees are trained to form a single stem, with small side branches at an angle, which promotes the formation of fruit over stem growth. Espalier trees are trained flat against a sunny wall, a technique which ensures the plants receive reflected heat, useful for peaches, pears and apricots.

❸ Bush fruit

Very rewarding because they tend to be highly productive, bush fruit are relatively small, many growing no taller than 1.2m (4ft), and much easier to manage than tree fruit. They are easy to prune and will produce enough produce in a small plot to make worthwhile quantities of jam; the fruit also freezes well for pies and desserts over winter. Most bush fruit thrive in cool summer climates too and in ordinary soil. However, blueberries will only flourish on acidic soil, so if rhododendrons and azaleas do well in your area, then they are worth a try; otherwise, if you are determined to grow them, consider a raised bed filled with compost-enriched, sandy, acidic topsoil. Recommended bush fruits include:

- Blackcurrants and redcurrants (pictured)
- Gooseberries
- Blueberries

❹ Cane fruit

Most of the berries fall into this category. Raspberries are easy to grow in a small garden, but they are not particularly attractive plants and need to be tied to supports. Many other berries form large plants and, given that they tend to be spiny too, are not ideal for small plots. However, breeders have created some smaller spineless cultivars, which may be worth a try. Fences and walls that receive sun for at least half the day are the best places to grow these plants, as they also offer a support to tie them to. Recommended cane fruits include:

- Raspberries – later-fruiting 'primocane' varieties are more vigorous and productive than traditional early to midsummer types
- Blackberries – spineless varieties are best for small plots (pictured)
- Tayberries and other hybrid berries – large but very productive plants
- Kiwi fruit – if you have sun and plenty of space

❺ Strawberries

In a category of their own, strawberries are ideal for the small garden and can even be grown in pots and windowboxes. 'Alpine' strawberries are the best choice for small gardens, as they do not produce runners like conventional strawberries, and instead tend to self-seed; they also have a long cropping season, and are popular with children, but their fruits are small. Conventional varieties tend to have a short season, and real strawberry-lovers will grow 'early', 'mid-season', and 'late' varieties; a viable alternative is one of the 'perpetual' types, which will produce fruit over many months. Recommended perpetual varieties include:

- 'Albion' (pictured)
- 'Buddy'
- 'Flamenco'
- 'Mara des Bois'

The home vegetable-growing revolution

The last few decades have seen a revolution in the way we think about growing vegetables at home. Vegetables can be beautiful! No longer pushed to the back of the garden out of sight, modern crops can be integrated into the garden as decorative elements. Chards, with their vivid red and yellow stems, the ferny foliage of carrots, and the flowers of runner beans are all easy to fit into planting schemes. But, in some cases, varieties recommended for their ornamental impact are not always as good for eating; the trendy black Tuscan kale, 'Cavolo Nero', is one such case and becomes horribly leathery if the leaves are left on the plant for too long.

The recent trend for 'mini veg' has resulted in a range of new varieties that harvest well when small, or are compact and easy to grow, and especially useful to the home gardener who has only containers or other confined spaces in which to raise their crops.

Growing young and mini veg

In many cases, you do not have to wait until vegetable plants are mature; young crops are often more tender and tastier. Many leafy vegetables can be cropped just a few weeks after sowing, when still large seedlings, which makes them ideal for impatient gardeners and those growing crops in small spaces. Choose from the following vegetables and techniques:

VEG TO HARVEST WHEN YOUNG
- Beetroot
- Carrot
- Kale
- Kohlrabi
- Leek
- Mooli - Asian radish
- Onion
- Pak choi
- Turnip

The following vegetables can be treated as 'cut and come again' crops. Allow the crop to grow a good supply of young tender leaves and then harvest them, leaving short stumps to regrow. Alternatively, harvest them leaf by leaf.

VEG FOR 'CUT AND COME AGAIN'
- Kale
- Leaf beet
- Swiss chard
- Lettuce
- Oriental greens
- Peas – grown for shoots
- Spinach

Choosing cultivars

Seed catalogues are full of different varieties, all of which may seem wonderful, so that even experienced gardeners can find it difficult to make the right choices. To help you decide what will suit you best, familiarise yourself with the terms used to describe vegetable crops.

• **Heritage varieties** If you are interested in garden history or growing crops your great-grandparents grew, try these. Although a few are worth growing quite apart from this interest, modern varieties are usually better.

• **F1 hybrids** Although relatively expensive, these often represent the best of modern breeding. A great advantage is that F1 plants are completely consistent, which is helpful if you have only a small space. The caveat is that inconsistency can be an advantage; for example, when crops that deteriorate quickly after they are ready to harvest, such as lettuce or broccoli, mature at different times.

• **Early cropping** This describes varieties that mature earlier than other crops of the same type. For leafy vegetables, this may mean they grow quickly, but for fruiting crops, like tomatoes, or root crops, such as potatoes, 'early' means they produce fruit, or tubers big enough to eat, earlier than other varieties. This trait is useful when growing a warm climate crop, such as tomatoes, in a cool-summer area.

• **Pest and disease resistance** This is a really crucial factor to consider. The old-fashioned use of chemical warfare to control pests and diseases is not appropriate today and many synthetic pesticides are banned for amateur use, making other methods of control vital. It is now possible to buy many vegetable varieties – often F1 hybrids – that are resistant to some of the major problem diseases and pests.

FAR LEFT Small vegetable plots need careful planning. Many of the crops here will be harvested when young, leaving space for others that will grow larger and need to remain in the ground for longer.

TOP RIGHT *Tagetes* add a splash of colour to a vegetable border and may reduce the impact of certain pests, while also attracting pollinators.

BOTTOM RIGHT Mooli, a radish from Asia, grows rapidly in late summer, and can be eaten raw, cooked, or made into Korean kimchi pickle.

Choosing a productive site

Fruit and vegetables are not like ornamental plants, many of which are very tolerant of infertile soils or poor conditions. The general rule for edible plants is that the more effort you put into maintaining a fertile soil, the more you get out, and this applies especially to vegetables. If your garden is shady, then realistically there is little you can do; if your soil is poor and/or dry, then conditions are far from ideal but as countless gardeners have done throughout history, it is possible to make improvements and reap the rewards.

Light requirements

Most tree fruit and vegetables, including brassicas and warm-summer crops like tomatoes, need full sunlight, although a few, notably leaf crops, perform better in partial shade. Fruits, including raspberries and strawberries, can be grown in very light shade, while blackberries will produce a reasonable crop in areas that receive just an hour or two of direct sunlight.

Crop choices for shade

In small urban gardens, shade cast by buildings can limit your crop options, but these will thrive in areas that are shaded for up to half the day.

- Beetroot
- Broad beans (pictured)
- Coriander
- Dill
- Leaf beets
- Oriental greens
- Parsley
- Peas, for shoots
- Salad leaf crops: lettuce, radish, rocket, spring onion
- Spinach
- Winter radish

FAR LEFT Kiwi fruit is a large-growing climber, and with care it can be trained along a wall or fence, but you will need both a male and a female plant for the fruit to form.

LEFT Runner beans can be successfully grown in large containers, such as old dustbins.
DESIGN BY GARDENS OF APPELTERN

RIGHT There is no getting away from it – growing vegetables involves work and good organisation. Here, the soil is being raked prior to sowing a salad crop.

Improving your soil

Poor soils can be improved or, if really bad, replaced, but if you are buying in topsoil, check your sources very carefully, as poor quality products are often sold to unsuspecting buyers – ask a landscaping company or garden designer if they can recommend a supplier.

Very sandy or heavy clay soils are best improved with composted material, which is now widely available as green waste from local government contractors, or you can add your own homemade compost. Compost breaks down over time into humus, which is vital for vegetable growing. Water and nutrients cling to humus, and it then releases them slowly into the soil, providing the perfect recipe for hungry crops. Traditionally, compost was dug into the soil, but this is no longer considered important, and may even damage some soils. Instead, spread a thick layer over the surface and let worms and invertebrates pull it down to build up a natural soil profile.

WHY GROW CROPS IN RAISED BEDS?

Raised beds have become very fashionable, and have many benefits for the vegetable grower, but they also have a few disadvantages.

Advantages:
- Fantastic if you have a bad back!
- Very good for attending to smaller vegetables that need intensive weeding or managing, such as dwarf beans and salad crops.
- The soil in them warms up quickly in spring.
- They demarcate growing areas, and help protect crops from children and some pets.
- They are essential if you are gardening on a hard surface and have no soil.

Disadvantages:
- The soil can heat up and dry out disastrously in warm weather.
- The soil is more likely to freeze in winter.
- The sides can act as barracks for armies of slugs and snails.
- Finding the soil for them can involve extensive and arguably unnecessary re-landscaping.
- They can be expensive and time-consuming to make.
- Why chop down trees to grow vegetables?

Protecting crops in tiny plots

Vegetable gardeners have always tried to extend the growing season by warming the soil and protecting their crops against the cold, practices that are now much easier thanks to a plethora of devices and materials, including cloches, frames, fleeces, polytunnels, and mini-tunnels. Many products are not exactly aesthetically pleasing, and this may influence the extent to which you want to use them in a small space where they cannot be hidden from view. However, others, such as bell cloches or cold frames that imitate Victorian styles, lend a retro elegance and can look attractive in a garden setting.

The big cover up

The easiest way to extend the growing season and to protect plants against flying pests is to cover them. Try the following methods:

- Spring starts a lot earlier if the soil is protected under a sheet of glass or clear plastic, allowing seeds and young plants to make quick progress.
- Half-hardy plants, such as tomatoes and peppers, can be protected from late frosts, *but only* if they are very light, with a covering of one or two layers of fleece or a similar insulating material.
- Young vegetable plants are very vulnerable to damage from birds, including domestic chickens. Keeping them under cover will protect them during these early stages, but it is no defence against snails or slugs, which may do just as much damage.
- In some cases, a physical cover will protect crops from aerial insect attack. An example is covering carrots to protect them from carrot fly, a low-flying pest whose grubs eat the roots. Cabbages and other brassicas must also be covered to prevent the cabbage white butterfly from laying eggs on them.

LEFT With a little ingenuity, you can successfully grow a wide variety of vegetables in pots on a balcony, if watered and fed regularly. DESIGN BY STELLA FABER

TOP RIGHT Crops can be protected by decorative old-fashioned bell jars, as used by 19th century gardeners.

BOTTOM RIGHT A mini mesh tunnel will protect young plants from birds and flying insect pests, and also provides light shade.

CASE STUDY: Compact productive plot

Design by Carol Whitehead

FAR LEFT Mary grows a wide range of vegetables, including broad beans, peas, mangetout peas, tomatoes, beetroot, chard, perpetual spinach, broccoli, and lettuce. Some crops, such as courgettes and herbs, do better in pots, the latter are easily swamped by larger-growing plants in the raised beds. There are some soft fruit bushes, including redcurrants and raspberries, with strawberries flourishing at ground level.

TOP LEFT Mary explains that her garden is not just a productive space and it looks good all year round. She uses it as an extra room outside to relax and entertain. The local wildlife is appreciative too, and wrens – great devourers of insect pests – have started to nest in the garden.

BOTTOM LEFT Slatted wooden trellis extends the wall height, increasing the vertical growing space. There is room for a passion flower (*Passiflora caerulea*), as well as a few apple cordons.

Mary Norton's small London garden is mainly given over to growing fruit and vegetables. Designer Carol Whitehead helped her to create a new plan for what was previously a lawn and small borders, and because Mary didn't want to bend too much, she included raised beds for the vegetable-growing areas, made from traditional bricks and filled with carefully selected imported soil. The planting style is completely different to a traditional vegetable garden where plants are grown in rows. Fruit and vegetables mingle here in a more integrated fashion, helping to disguise some crops, which at certain phases of their life cycle can look rather unattractive, while ensuring the garden looks good year-round.

PRODUCTIVE AND ORNAMENTAL PLANTS

1. Runner beans
2. *Wisteria sinensis*
3. Cordon tomatoes
4. *Epimedium* x *perralchicum* 'Fröhnleiten'
5. Lemon verbena
6. Tomatoes (front) and a blackcurrant
7. Chives and cherry tomatoes in a pot
8. Passion flower (*Passiflora caerulea*)

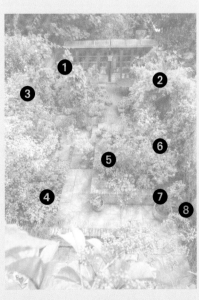

GARDEN DIMENSIONS: approx 22m x 8m (72ft x 26ft)

LEFT Figs can produce a worthwhile and delicious crop on a sunny wall. However, they are greedy plants and need feeding well, and they can potentially grow very large, so rigorous pruning may be needed. Adventurous gardeners could seek out *Ficus afghanistanica*, which is smaller-growing.

LEFT Traditionally, crops were rotated around the growing area to prevent a build-up of pests and diseases. This is difficult in a small garden, but fortunately this practice is not essential for the majority of vegetable varieties, particularly when many different types are grown together. Here, young tomato plants are scaling bamboo canes.

Plant selector

Just as many enthusiastic gardeners try to squeeze as many plants into their plot as they can, this plant selector is a similar attempt to cram as much useful information into a small space as possible! I have included most plants mentioned in the book, and provided basic information about their appearance, size, main seasons of interest, and the conditions they need to thrive. For ease of use, the plants are split into their plant categories: trees, shrubs, sub-shrubs, perennials, grasses, climbers and bulbs.

I have used abbreviations in the listings in order to make most effective use of the space – these, and my terminology are explained below.

LEFT *Hydrangea paniculata* 'Grandiflora', *Verbena bonariensis* and *Perovskia* 'Blue Spire' conspire in a pastel confection.

RIGHT The acid colours of spring-flowering *Euphorbia epithymoides* add interest at ground level.

HOW TO USE THE PLANT SELECTOR
KEY TO ABBREVIATIONS

HEIGHT IN METRES (FEET AND INCHES)
Trees and shrubs: ultimate height is given.
Perennials: height achieved annually.
For perennials with flowers on tall stems, two figures are given separated by an forward slash: e.g. 0.5/2.0: the first height is for foliage/second for flower stems

SPREAD IN METRES (FEET AND INCHES)
Trees, shrubs, sub-shrubs: ultimate spread is given.
Perennials: figure refers to the base of the plant, not the top growth, after three years; many will continue to spread wider and this is referred to in the notes if it is extensive.
Climbers: maximum projection from a vertical support.

FLOWERS
Since entries often cover a number of species and garden varieties, a range of flower colours may be mentioned.

FOLIAGE
E = evergreen

SEASON OF INTEREST
This generally refers to the main season of interest, normally the flowering period, unless the plant is grown mainly for its foliage. However, many species grown primarily for flowers also have attractive foliage, and sometimes seed-head interest too; this is noted if it is particularly good.
Spr = spring
Su = summer
ESu = early summer
MSu = midsummer
LSu = late summer
Aut = autumn
Win = winter
All = all year

LIGHT
S = sun
LSh = light shade
Sh = full shade

OTHER SOIL AND SITE CONDITIONS
M = needs moist (but not wet) soil
(M) = flourishes in moist soil but copes in drier conditions
D = drought tolerant
Ac = needs neutral to acid soil
Ø = dislikes full sun or wind exposure
Ex = good in exposed environments, often including coastal

HARDINESS
Any system of categorising plant hardiness is problematic, and has exceptions. The global standard, developed by the United States Department of Agriculture, sets out a series of 'zones' which express the minimum winter temperature at which a plant can survive. A simplified version relevant to the plants in this book is used here. Where a range is given (e.g. 5–6), there is variation between the species available.

Zone	minimum temperature
2	from -46°C to -40°C (-55°F to -40°F)
3	from -40°C to -33°C (-40°F to - 27°F)
4	from -34°C to -28°C (-27°F to -18°F)
5	from -28°C to -23°C (-18°F to -9°F)
6	from -23°C to -17°C (-9°F to 1°F)
7	from -17°C to -12°C (1°F to 10°F)
8	from -12°C to -6°C (10°F to 21°F)
9	from -6°C to -1°C (21°F to 30°F)

An asterisk * in the height or spread column refers to additional information in the Notes.

NAME	DESCRIPTION					CULTIVATION			NOTES
	HEIGHT M (FT)	SPREAD M (FT)	FLOWERS/FRUIT	FOLIAGE	SEASON OF INTEREST	LIGHT	OTHER	HARD-INESS	
TREES									
Acer griseum	6.0 (20)	3.0 (10)	inconspicuous	small, attractive	All	S, LSh	Ø	4	peeling cinnamon-coloured bark
Acer palmatum, many varieties	5.0 (16)	5.0 (16)	inconspicuous	divided, attractive	Spr, Aut	S, LSh	Ø	5	also many dwarf forms; wide variation in leaf colour and shape
Albizia julibrissin	10.0 (33)	10.0 (33)	pink fluffy	divided, attractive	Spr	S	Ø	6	good tree for urban gardens
Catalpa bignonioides 'Aurea'	6.0* (20)	3.0 (10)	white	yellow-tinged	ESu	S, LSh	Ø	5	* height varies depending on height of graft
Cercis canadensis 'Forest Pansy'	9.0 (30)	9.0 (30)	bright pink	dark red-tinged	Spr	S, LSh	Ø	4	other *Cercis* species also good
Crataegus species	6.0 (20)	6.0 (20)	white, pink	small, neat	Spr–ESu, Aut	S, LSh	Ex	3-4	wide range of species, all can be kept clipped
Eucalyptus species	20.0* (66)	6.0 (20)	usually insignificant	E, blue-grey	All	S	Ex	8	* only suitable if regularly coppiced
Malus – crab types	8.0 (26)	6.0 (20)	white, pink, fruit various colours	medium-sized	Spr, Aut	S, LSh		4	grown mainly for fruit but flowers can also be spectacular
Malus tschonoskii	12.0 (39)	4.0 (13)	white	neat shape, autumn colour	Spr, Aut	S		4	grown mainly for tight pyramidical shape
Mespilus germanica	3.0 (10)	5.0 (16)	white	neat shape, autumn colour	Spr	S		5	interesting and potentially edible fruit
Prunus – flowering	8.0* (26)	8.0 (26)	white, pink	autumn colour	Spr, Aut	S, LSh		4-5	* height varies depending on variety
Prunus cerasifera 'Nigra', *P. x cistena*	8.0 (26)	5.0 (16)	white	dark purple	Spr, Aut	S		4	can be messy in time, sometimes grown as hedging
Pyrus salicifolia 'Pendula'	12.0 (39)	9.0 (30)	white	silver	Spr, Aut	S	Ex	4	arching habit, can be clipped
Rhus typhina	6.0 (20)	6.0 (20)	dark red 'candles'	divided, light	Spr, Aut	S, LSh		3	suckers can be a problem, can be coppiced
Sorbus species	10.0* (33)	5.0 (16)	white, fruit can be red, yellow, white, pink	divided, attractive	Spr & Aut	S	Ex	3*	* height and hardiness vary depending on species
Stewartia species	10.0 (33)	5.0 (16)	white	good autumn colour	Su, Aut	S, LSh	Ø	5	good choice for coastal gardens
SHRUBS									
Abelia x grandiflora	1.2 (4)	2.0 (7)	pink/white	small, darkish	ESu–MSu	S, Lsh		5	compact grower
Abutilon species	2.0 (7)	1.0 (39")	yellow, pink, red	light green	ESu–Aut	S		8	very long-flowering
Aloysia citrodora	3.0* (10)	3.0 (10)	white, small	narrow leaves, intense lemon aroma	Su	S		8	* easily kept much smaller; usually grown as a pot plant to be overwintered inside
Amelanchier species	6.0 (20)	4.0 (13)	white, dark purple fruit	good autumn colour	Spr & Aut	S, LSh	(M)	2-4	fruit popular with birds

Acer palmatum 'Osakazuki'

Albizia julibrissin

Catalpa bignonioides 'Aurea'

Prunus 'Shogetsu'

Abelia x grandiflora 'Francis Mason'

SHRUBS

NAME	DESCRIPTION					CULTIVATION			NOTES
	HEIGHT M (FT)	SPREAD M (FT)	FLOWERS/FRUIT	FOLIAGE	SEASON OF INTEREST	LIGHT	OTHER	HARD-INESS	
Aralia elata	4.0 (13)	2.5 (8)	white	large, divided	Spr–Aut	S, LSh		4	exotic looking, distinctive
Aronia species	2.0 (7)	2.0 (7)	white, dark purple fruit	good autumn colour	Spr & Aut	S, LSh		3	fruit makes good jam
Atriplex halimus	1.5 (5)	1.5 (5)	insignificant	silver	Spr–Aut	S	D, Ex	8	good for coastal sites
Baccharis patagonica	3.0 (10)	3.0 (10)	small, white	E, dense	MSu	S	D, Ex	8	good for coastal sites
Berberis thunbergii	3.0 (10)	3.0 (10)	small, yellow	available in several colour forms	Spr–Aut	S		4	dwarf and upright forms available
Betula nana	2.0 (7)	2.0 (7)	small catkins	small, neat	Spr–Aut	S	Ex	2	attractive dwarf foliage shrub
Buddleja davidii	4.0 (13)	4.0 (13)	purple, also pink or white	slightly grey-silver	MSu–LSu	S	D	4	very good for butterflies, can be treated as herbaceous in cold areas
Bupleurum fruticosum	2.0 (7)	2.0 (7)	yellow clusters	E, glossy	All	S		7	good for coastal sites
Buxus sempervirens	4.0 (13)	3.0 (10)	insignificant	E, neat, glossy	All	S, LSh	D	5	the best shrub for clipping
Ceanothus species	4.0 (13)	4.0 (13)	blue	E, slightly grey	ESu	S	D	7	fast-growing, but may need pruning; good by coast but not cold exposure
Choisya species	2.0 (7)	2.0 (7)	white	E, glossy	ESu	S, Sh	D	7	neat, rounded shape
Cornus alternifolia 'Argentea'	5.0 (16)	4.0 (13)	white	white/green variegated, small	ESu–Aut	S, LSh		3	valuable for illuminating light shade
Coronilla valentina subsp. *glauca*	2.0 (7)	2.0 (7)	yellow pea-like flowers	E, neat, greyish	Win–Spr	S		8	valuable but short-lived
Corylus maxima 'Purpurea'	6.0 (20)	6.0 (20)	spring catkins	deep purple	Spr–Aut	S, LSh		5	good for coppicing
Cotinus coggygria 'Royal Purple'	6.0 (20)	6.0 (20)	smoke-like plumes	purple, rounded	Spr–Aut	S, LSh		5	good for coppicing
Cotoneaster species	*	*	white, red fruit in autumn	dark neat, some are evergreen	Spr & Aut	S, LSh		4-6	* very wide range of sizes, all good for pollinators
Daphne species	1.0* (39")	1.0 (39")	white, pink, heavily scented	E, dark, dense	Spr	S, LSh		4-6	* size varies according to species, slow-growing
Elaeagnus x ebbingei, *E. pungens*	3.0 (10)	3.0 (10)	inconspicuous but scented	E, many forms variegated	All	S, LSh		6	wide range of varieties
Enkianthus species	3.0 (10)	3.0 (10)	white/pink bell-shaped	E, dark	Spr	S, LSh	Ac, Ø	6	good for bees
Escallonia species	3.0 (10)	3.0 (10)	red, pink	E, dark, small leaves	Spr–MSu	S, LSh		8	easily pruned to size, good for coastal sites
Euonymus fortunei and *E. japonicus*, many varieties	0.6 (2)	3.0 (10)	insignificant	E, many silver or gold variegated forms	All	S, Sh		5-7	sprawling but can also climb

Amelanchier lamarckii

Buddleja davidii 'Nanho Blue'

Cotoneaster x suecicus 'Coral Beauty'

Daphne mezereum

Elaeagnus x ebbingei

NAME	DESCRIPTION					CULTIVATION			NOTES
	HEIGHT M (FT)	SPREAD M (FT)	FLOWERS/FRUIT	FOLIAGE	SEASON OF INTEREST	LIGHT	OTHER	HARD-INESS	
SHRUBS									
Euphorbia mellifera	2.0 (7)	2.5 (8)	pale green, fragrant	E, neat mound of light green	Spr	S, LSh		8	
Fothergilla species	3.0 (10)	3.0 (10)	white, fluffy	good autumn colour	Spr & Aut	LSh	Ac, Ø	5	slow growing
Fuchsia magellanica and hybrids	4.0 (13)	3.0 (10)	red, pink	E, but can lose leaves in cold	Su	S, LSh		7	good by the coast, eventual size reached only in mild areas
Hamamelis mollis	5.0 (16)	5.0 (16)	yellow, scented	good autumn colour	Win–Spr, Aut	S, LSh	Ø	4	slow-growing
Hibiscus syriacus	3.0 (10)	2.0 (7)	pink, white, blue	yellow autumn colour	Su & Aut	S		5	best in areas with warm summer climates
Hydrangea species	3.0 (10)	3.0 (10)	pink, white, blue, fading attractively	large, rather coarse	MSu-LSu	S, LSh	M	5	good by the coast, easily pruned, many varieties; blue forms need acid soil
Ilex species	6.0* (20)	4.0 (13)	insignificant, grown for foliage and berries	E, dark, spiny, many variegated varieties	All	S, Sh		6	* height depends on variety, only female varieties have berries
Juniperus scopulorum 'Skyrocket'	3.0 (10)	0.8 (32")	insignificant	E, grey	All	S		2	dramatic columnar shape
Laurus nobilis	5.0 (16)	4.0 (13)	insignificant	E, glossy, aromatic	All	S, Sh		8	leaves can be used in cooking; can be clipped
Ligustrum ovalifolium varieties	6.0 (20)	6.0 (20)	cream, clusters	E, but can lose leaves in cold	All	S, LSh		5	needs to establish before flowering; also some variegated varieties
Lonicera nitida	2.0 (7)	4.0 (13)	insignificant	E, very small, neat, dense	All	S, LSh	Ex	7	can be clipped as a box substitute.
Mahonia x media 'Charity'	5.0 (16)	3.0 (10)	yellow, scented	E, divided, holly-like	Win–Spr	S, LSh		7	slow growing, many similar varieties
Myrtus communis	4.0 (13)	4.0 (13)	white	E, small, neat, aromatic	All	S		8	slow-growing
Nandina domestica	1.5 (5)	2.0 (7)	white, in clusters, red fruit	divided, elegant	MSu & Aut	S, LSh		7	best in warm summer climates
Osmanthus species	4.0 (13)	4.0 (13)	white, heavily scented	E, usually small	Spr	LSh		7	foliage is main difference between species
Philadelphus coronarius 'Aureus'	2.0 (7)	1.5 (5)	white, heavily scented	yellow-green	ESu	LSh		5	a less vigorous variety of a normally large shrub
Photinia x fraseri	4.0 (13)	4.0 (13)	white, but not conspicuous	E, strong red in spring	Spr	S, LSh		8	can be clipped as a hedge
Physocarpus opulifolius	2.5 (8)	2.5 (8)	white	purple- or yellow-tinged varieties	Spr–Aut	S, LSh	D	2	compact habit
Pieris species	3.0 (10)	3.0 (10)	white, bell-shaped	E, very strong red in spring	All	LSh	Ac, Ø	6	vulnerable to late frosts

Fuchsia magellanica var *gracilis*

Hamamelis mollis var *pallida*

Nandina domestica

Osmanthus x burkwoodii

Philadelphus 'Belle Etoile'

NAME	DESCRIPTION					CULTIVATION			NOTES
	HEIGHT M (FT)	SPREAD M (FT)	FLOWERS/FRUIT	FOLIAGE	SEASON OF INTEREST	LIGHT	OTHER	HARD -INESS	
SHRUBS									
Pittosporum tenuifolium	6.0* (20)	3.0 (10)	insignificant but scented	E, neat, various colours	All	S		8	* size varies according to variety; some good compact forms
Prunus lusitanica	5.0 (16)	4.0 (13)	white clusters	E, glossy, neat	All	S, Sh		7	classic evergreen, can be clipped
Pyracantha species	4.0 (13)	3.0 (10)	white, spectacular fruit: red, orange, yellow	compact habit, easily clipped	Aut–Win	S, LSh		5	often kept clipped as a wall shrub
Rhamnus alaternus 'Argenteovariegata'	5.0 (16)	4.0 (13)	inconspicuous	E, small, variegated	All	S, Sh		7	compact, upright habit
Rhododendron – 'Japanese azalea' types	1.0 (39")	1.2 (4)	purple, pink, white – very bright	E, neat, dense growth habit	Spr	S, LSh	Ac	6-7	can be clipped as a hedge, but flowering will be reduced
Rhododendron – deciduous azalea types	2.5 (8)	2.0 (7)	yellow, orange, white, most heavily scented	light green	Spr–ESu	S, LSh	Ac	5-6	spectacular but flowering season only 3 weeks
Rhododendron species	*	*	various	E, varying in size	Win–ESu	S, LSh	Ac	5-7	* very wide range, many dwarf-growing but choose carefully for size
Ribes sanguineum	3.0 (10)	2.5(8)	pink	upright habit	Spr	S, LSh		6	easily pruned to size
Rosa	*	*	any colour but blue, some have attractive hips	rarely attractive	ESu–LSu	S, LSh		5-7	* very wide range, vast number of varieties
Salix lanata	0.9 (3)	1.5 (5)	insignificant	silver-grey and downy	Spr- Aut	S		2	one of many possible species
Sarcococca species	1.5 (5)	2.0 (7)	insignificant, but heavily scented	E, narrow, glossy	Win	LSh-Sh		6	slow, but rewarding
Skimmia japonica	1.0 (39")	1.0 (39")	white, clusters; red berries	E, shiny mid-green	All, but Win best	S, LSh	Ac	7	good ground cover
Spiraea japonica 'Gold Flame'; *S. japonica* 'Golden Princess'	0.6 (2)	0.6 (2)	pink-red	yellow-tinged	ESu	S, LSh		3	very useful compact shrubs
Syringa meyeri	1.5 (5)	1.2 (4)	pink, clusters	small, attractive	ESu	S, LSh		4	one of several small-growing lilacs
Teucrium chamaedrys	0.6 (2)	0.8 (32")	pink flower clusters	E, small, dense	All	S		5	often clipped to form a low hedge
Viburnum x bodnantense	3.5 (12)	3.0 (10)	pink, slight scent	attractive texture	Win–Spr	S, LSh		7	upright habit; months of winter flowers
Viburnum x carlcephalum	3.0 (10)	2.0 (7)	white, heavily scented	rounded	ESu	S, LSh		5	several similar scented species

Pyracantha 'Navaho'

Rhododendron 'Freya'

Rosa 'Zéphirine Drouhin'

Skimmia japonica 'Thereza'

Syringa pubescens subsp microphylla 'Superba'

NAME	DESCRIPTION					CULTIVATION			NOTES
	HEIGHT M (FT)	SPREAD M (FT)	FLOWERS/FRUIT	FOLIAGE	SEASON OF INTEREST	LIGHT	OTHER	HARD-INESS	
SHRUBS									
Viburnum davidii	1.5 (5)	2.2 (7' 6")	white, dark purple fruit	E, dense	All	S, LSh		6	very good ground cover
Viburnum tinus	4.0 (13)	3.0 (10)	white, clusters	E, glossy, mid-green	Win–Spr	S, LSh		7	can be clipped
Yucca species	1.5/3.0 (5/10)	2.0 (7)	white in spectacular spike	E, spiky rosette	Su	S		5-8	flower spikes rarely produced; hardiness varies between species
SUB-SHRUBS									
Artemisia abrotanum	0.9 (3)	0.9 (3)	inconspicuous	finely divided, grey-green, heavily aromatic	Spr–Aut	S	D, Ex	4	can be kept smaller by occasional pruning
Ballota pseudodictamnus	0.5 (20")	0.8 (32")	inconspicuous	E, densely woolly, grey, aromatic	Spr–Aut	S	D	8	technically a sub-shrub but better cut back hard in autumn
Calluna vulgaris and *Erica* species (heathers)	0.5–1.0 (20"–39")	0.5 (20")	white, pink	E, very small, densely packed, often purple or grey	depending on species: Win or MSu – Aut	S	Ac, Ex	4-7	*Erica carnea* is lime-tolerant, but none thrive on heavy or damp soils
Cistus species	0.5–2.0 (20"–7')	0.8–2.0 (32"–7')	white, pink	E, aromatic	ESu	S	D	7-8	species vary greatly in size and habit, all can be short-lived
Convolvulus cneorum	0.5 (20")	0.9 (3)	white, open	E, grey and silky	All	S	D	8	dense, sprawling habit, mainly grown for foliage
Cytisus hybrid varieties	1.5 (5)	1.0 (39")	yellow, orange, red	E, small leaves on green stems	ESu	S	D	5	quick-growing, spectacular but short-lived
Hebe, smaller species	2.0 (7)	1.0 (39")	white or purple-blue, some pink	E, often grey or pink-tinged	All	S		7-8	extensive and varied group, particularly useful by sea, but dislike cold; some grown for foliage, others for flowers
Hebe cupressoides	1.0 (39")	1.0 (39")	white, small	E, green, tiny, dense	All	S		7	one of many compact sub-shrubs grown for foliage
Helichrysum italicum subsp *serotinum*	0.6 (2)	0.8 (32")	yellow, small	E, silver, spicy scent	All	S	D, Ex	7	can get untidy with time, but hard spring pruning can rejuvenate
Lavandula species	1.0 (39")	1.0 (39")	purple, mauve	E, silvery or grey, heavily aromatic	ESu–MSu	S	D	5-8	light pruning after flowering essential to keep shape; wide range of varieties and hardiness
Perovskia atriplicifolia	1.2 (4)	0.4 (16")	purple	fine, silvery, aromatic	MSu	S	D	5	tough semi-desert plant, with good winter form; usually pruned to ground in spring; upright shape

Viburnum davidii

Artemisia abrotanum

Cytisus scoparius

Hebe 'Pink Pixie'

Perovskia 'Blue Spire'

NAME	DESCRIPTION					CULTIVATION			NOTES
	HEIGHT M (FT)	SPREAD M (FT)	FLOWERS/FRUIT	FOLIAGE	SEASON OF INTEREST	LIGHT	OTHER	HARD-INESS	
SUB-SHRUBS									
Phlomis species	1.2 (4)	1.0 (39")	yellow, purple	E, silvery	ESu	S	D	7-8	underrated but good for hot dry and coastal locations
Potentilla fruticosa	1.2 (4)	1.0 (39")	yellow, orange, white	dense, small leaves	MSu	S	D, Ex	3	the hardiest sub-shrub but deciduous
Rosmarinus officinalis	1.2 (4)	1.0 (39")	blue	E, needle-like, aromatic	MSu	S	D	6	variable size/shape depending on variety
Ruta graveolens	1.0 (39")	1.0 (39")	yellow, small	grey, divided, neat	ESu	S	D	5	foliage can irritate skin, so beware!
Salix – dwarf forms	1.5 (5)	2.0 (7)	catkin-like	often grey	Su	S		2-5	varied group with a great range of sizes, can be hard pruned when too big
Santolina chamaecyparissus	0.5 (20")	0.7 (27")	yellow buttons	green or silver-grey	Su	S	D	7	spectacular but often short-lived
PERENNIALS									
Acanthus spinosus	1.0/1.7 (39"/ 5' 7")	1.0 (39")	white/purple	dark, divided, emerges early in mild winters	Spr–LSu	S, LSh	D	6	slow to establish, but hard to get rid of, as roots continually regenerate
Achillea, many varieties	0.8 (32")	0.4 (16")	everything but blue; mostly yellows and reds	dark, very finely divided, aromatic	MSu–LSu	S	D	3-5	many varieties short-lived
Agapanthus varieties	0.4/1.0 (16"/ 39")	0.6 (2)	blues, purples, whites	strap-like, low	MSu–LSu	S	D	7-8	very wide range now available and hardier than often thought
Agastache rugosa	0.8 (32")	0.4 (16")	purple, blue spikes	very minty aromatic	MSu–LSu	S, LSh		7	short-lived; good seed heads
Ajuga - many varieties	0.2 (8")	0.5 (20")	small blue	semi-E, dark, glossy, broad	Spr	LSh	(M), Ø	5	a number of varieties; selected mainly for leaf colour
Amsonia species	0.9 (3)	0.5 (20")	blue, metallic look	linear, on erect stems, good autumn colour	ESu	S		4-7	slow to establish, but long-lived and reliable
Anaphalis species	0.8 (32")	0.6 (2)	white, papery, everlasting	silvery, erect stems	MSu–LSu	S		3-5	long-lived and rewarding, does not spread
Anthemis punctata subsp *cupaniana*	0.3 (12")	1.0 (39")	white daisies	silvery, low sprawling habit	MSu	S	D	6	good for covering a sunny bank
Artemisia stelleriana	0.4 (16")	0.4 (16")	inconspicuous	silvery, felty, divided, aromatic	Spr-Aut	S	D	3	sunny border gap-filler
Arum italicum 'Pictum'	0.3 (12")	0.4 (16")	arum lily type, bright red berries	glossy dark green with white markings	Win–ESu & LSu	LSh-Sh		6	summer dormant
Aruncus dioicus 'Kneiffii'	0.7 (27")	0.7 (27")	white plumes	very finely divided	ESu	S-LSh		3	space-filler for shade

Ruta graveolens

Santolina chamaecyparissus 'Nana'

Achillea 'Feuerland'

Ajuga reptans 'Catlin's Giant'

Anaphalis triplinervis

NAME	DESCRIPTION					CULTIVATION			NOTES
	HEIGHT (M)	SPREAD (M)	FLOWERS/FRUIT	FOLIAGE	SEASON OF INTEREST	LIGHT	OTHER	HARD-INESS	
PERENNIALS									
Aster divaricatus	0.7 (27")	0.6 (2)	white daisies	fresh green on dark stems	LSu–Aut	S-LSh		4	clumps will spread, good for edge of tree canopy
Aster x frikartii	0.7 (27")	0.6 (2)	lavender-purple daisies	mid-green	LSu–Aut	S		4	long flowering season
Astilbe varieties	0.6–0.8 (24"–32")	0.6 (2)	white, purple, pink stiff plumes	divided, dark	ESu–MSu	S-LSh	M	6	only really successful if they never dry out
Astrantia major	0.7 (27")	0.5 (20")	white, pink, red	divided	MSu–Aut	S-LSh	Ø	6	notable long flowering season, may self-seed in cooler, wetter areas
Bergenia species	0.4 (16")	0.6 (2)	white, pink	E, rounded, often purple in winter	Spr	S-Sh		3-7	very useful ground cover, slowly spreading
Brunnera macrophylla	0.5 (20")	0.7 (27")	blue, small	broad, coarse, dark	Spr	LSh		3	can spread, good below shrubs
Centranthus ruber	0.8 (32")	0.4 (16")	red, pink	glossy	MSu	S	D	6	does not spread but can self-seed strongly
Ceratostigma species	0.5 (20")	0.5 (20")	clear blue	often good autumn colour	LSu–Aut	S		6	slowly spreading, semi-woody
Chelone species	0.9 (3)	0.5 (20")	pink or white	dark, upright stems	LSu–Aut	S-LSh	(M)	3	spreads slowly to form large clumps
Chrysanthemum species	0.8 (32")	0.5 (20")	pink, yellow	divided	Aut	S		5	this information refers to the hardy garden varieties; many are short-lived
Convallaria majalis	0.2 (8")	0.4 (16")	white, heavily scented	simple, upright, wide leaves	Spr	LSh-Sh		3	classic spring flower, slow to start but eventually spreading
Crocosmia species	1.0 (39")	0.3 (12")	yellow, orange, red	upright sword-shaped	LSu–Aut	S-LSh		7	size, vigour and hardiness all vary
Cynara cardunculus	0.6/2.5 (2/8)	1.0 (39")	blue	silver leaves in late winter	Win–MSu	S		6	very large, but early foliage is exceptionally good
Dahlia varieties	0.5–2.0* (20"–7')	0.7 (27")	various, but never blue	divided, lush, sometimes dark	MSu–Aut	S		9	* height depends on variety; often needs winter protection
Darmera peltata	1.2 (4)	1.0 (39")	large pink heads before leaves emerge	dinner plate-size and shape	Spr & ESu–Aut	S-LSh	M	6	needs very damp ground to thrive; large and spreading but very effective if contained
Dianthus varieties	0.2–0.6* (8"–2')	0.2 (8")	white, pink, often scented	E, grey, some smaller species forming cushions	Spr–ESu	S	D	4	* size varies depending on species, best on well-drained limy soils

Aster x frikartii 'Mönch'

Astrantia 'Roma'

Brunnera macrophylla 'Dawson's White'

Ceratostigma plumbaginoides

Convallaria majalis

NAME	DESCRIPTION					CULTIVATION			NOTES
	HEIGHT (M)	SPREAD (M)	FLOWERS/FRUIT	FOLIAGE	SEASON OF INTEREST	LIGHT	OTHER	HARD-INESS	
PERENNIALS									
Diascia varieties	0.4* (16")	0.6 (2)	pink, profuse, can be long-flowering	small, heart-shaped, compact, low sprawling habit	ESu–Aut	S		8*	* size and hardiness vary according to species; fast-growing, compact and sprawling but short-lived
Dicentra species	0.3–1.0* (12"–39")	0.4 (16")	pink, white, often heart-shaped	fine, lush-looking	Spr	LSh–Sh	Ø	5	* size varies according to species, smaller ones most reliable and eventually spreading
Dierama species	0.6–1.5* (2–5)	0.5 (20")	pink, red, white bells on long arching stems	E, narrow arching, in clumps	Msu–LSu	S		7	* size varies according to species but most are tall, very elegant plants
Digitalis species	0.3/1.2 (12"/4')	0.4 (16")	pink, yellow, fawn	rosettes of broad leaves	ESu	S, LSh		5	the pink *D. purpurea* is largest, others are smaller and more graceful, and mostly yellow-fawn
Echinacea purpurea varieties	1.0 (39")	0.4 (16")	pink	broad, forms narrow clump	MSu–Aut	S		3	*E. purpurea* is the most reliable; but longevity still can be a problem
Epimedium species	0.3 (12")	0.4 (16")	yellow, white, pink	glossy, attractive, some species evergreen	Spr	LSh–Sh		5	traditional species very good ground cover; Asian species do not spread well but have better flowers
Eryngium bourgatii	0.5 (20")	0.4 (16")	blue/grey, spiny	divided, grey, attractive clumps	MSu	S	D	5	effective structural plant
Erysimum 'Bowles's Mauve'	0.9 (3)	0.8 (32")	soft mauve-purple	linear, greyish	Spr–MSu	S	D	6	bushy plant shape; very long flowering, but short-lived
Euphorbia amygdaloides var *robbiae*	0.6 (2)	0.8 (32")	yellow-green	E, dark, glossy	Win–Spr	S–Sh		7	can spread strongly; makes good cover for shady gardens
Euphorbia characias	1.5 (5)	1.5 (5)	yellow-green	E, greyish, rounded plant shape	Win–Spr	S, LSh	D	8	dead stems often need removing, good complement to bulbs
Geranium endressii, G. x oxonianum varieties	0.6 (2)	0.6 (2)	pink – various shades	forms rounded clumps but may collapse after flowering	ESu & Aut	S, LSh		5	very free-flowering, vigorous, potentially spreading
Geranium x magnificum	0.6 (2)	0.6 (2)	blue-purple	forms rounded clumps	ESu	S, LSh		5	old favourite, but still worth growing
Geum triflorum	0.4 (16")	0.4 (16")	yellow, small; fluffy seed heads	ferny looking	ESu–MSu	S	D	4	one of the earliest plants for seed head interest
Gillenia trifoliata	1.2 (4)	0.6 (2)	white, profuse	narrow, elegant; red stems	ESu	S, LSh		4	white flowers best against a dark background

Digitalis ferruginea

Epimedium x youngianum 'Niveum'

Erysimum 'Bowles's Mauve'

Euphorbia characias subsp *wulfenii*

Geranium x cantabrigiense 'Cambridge'

NAME	DESCRIPTION					CULTIVATION			NOTES
	HEIGHT M (FT)	SPREAD M (FT)	FLOWERS/FRUIT	FOLIAGE	SEASON OF INTEREST	LIGHT	OTHER	HARD -INESS	
PERENNIALS									
Helleborus x hybridus	0.6 (24")	0.8 (32")	red, yellow, grey, purple-black	E, divided	Spr	S, LSh		5	one of the most highly valued 'end of winter' flowers
Hemerocallis, smaller varieties	0.6 (24")	0.6 (2)	yellow, pink, red, brown	linear, tight clumps	ESu–MSu	S		5	very long-lived and resilient, but choose small varieties
Hesperantha coccinea	0.8 (32")	0.3 (12")	red, pink, white	linear, upright, in clumps	Aut	S	(M)	6	attractive in mild winter areas, untidy elsewhere
Heuchera varieties	0.3/0.7 (12"/27")	0.4 (16")	white, some red	many colours now available: yellow, purple, red	Spr–Aut	S, LSh		5	good for long-season interest but short-lived unless heavily mulched
Hosta, smaller varieties	0.3/0.8 (12"/32")	0.5 (20")	pale purple, white	wide, often variegated, sometimes blue-grey	Spr–Aut	LSh	M, Ø	6	popular foliage plants and available in many sizes; some will spread strongly in time
Hyssopus officinalis	0.6–0.8 (24"–32")	0.3 (12")	spikes of violet	small, aromatic, E in mild winters	ESu	S		4	almost shrubby habit, can be kept compact with light pruning
Iris foetidissima	0.7 (27")	0.4 (16")	yellow, small; orange berries	E, green, linear	ESu & Win	Sh	D	6	dull but thrives in dry shade
Iris: dwarf bearded varieties	0.3 (12")	0.2 (8")	wide variety of colours, but short flowering season	grey, sword-like	ESu	S	D	3	very varied group
Kirengeshoma palmata	0.9 (3)	0.6 (2)	pale yellow bells	maple-like	MSu	LSh–Sh		5	very distinguished, slow to establish but long-lived
Kniphofia 'Little Maid'	0.6 (24")	0.5 (20")	pale yellow, in spikes	linear, tight clumps	MSu	S		8	one of the few smaller varieties of these dramatic plants
Libertia species	0.7 (27")	0.5 (20")	white	linear, tight clumps	MSu	S, LSh		8	long-lived in milder climates
Limonium platyphyllum	0.3–0.8 (12'–32")	0.5 (20")	tiny violet flowers in huge heads	glossy, paddle-like	MSu–LSu	S	D, Ex	5	long-lived, non-spreading, unusual
Liriope and *Ophiopogon* species	0.3 (12")	0.3 (12")	violet spikes; purple or black berries	E, linear, almost grass-like; one form is black	flowers Aut, foliage all year	LSh, Sh		5	slowly forms dense mats; much faster in warm humid summer climates
Lunaria rediviva	0.8 (32")	0.4 (16")	very pale violet, scented; papery seed heads	stiff clump	Spr	LSh		5	long flowering season
Lythrum species	1.5 (5)	0.3 (12")	vivid magenta spikes	small leaves, stiff upright habit	MSu–LSu	S, LSh	(M)	3	can seed aggressively if near wetland outside region of origin

Helleborus x hybridus

Hosta nakaiana

Kirengeshoma palmata

Liriope muscari 'Gold Band'

Lunaria rediviva

NAME	DESCRIPTION					CULTIVATION			NOTES
	HEIGHT M (FT)	SPREAD M (FT)	FLOWERS/FRUIT	FOLIAGE	SEASON OF INTEREST	LIGHT	OTHER	HARD -INESS	
PERENNIALS									
Mathiasella bupleuroides	1.0 (39")	0.6 (2)	green	divided	Spr–ESu	S		8	old flowers continue to look attractive, unusual
Mentha species	0.6 (2)	0.5 (20")	pale purple spikes	aromatic	ESu	S, LSh	(M)	6	spreads aggressively, used as culinary herb
Nepeta x *faassenii*	0.6 (2)	0.9 (3)	violet	greyish green	ESu & Aut	S	D	3	sprawling habit; repeat flowers if pruned after first flush, many similar varieties
Penstemon varieties	0.5–1.0 (20'–39")	0.4 (16")	pink, red, purple	narrow leaves	LSu–Aut	S		6-8	wide range of colour and size; prune hard in spring; sometimes untidy habit
Persicaria amplexicaulis	0.6–1.2 (2–4)	0.9 (3)	pink, red	large leaves, neat mound forming habit	MSu–LSu	S, LSh	(M)	4	smaller varieties increasingly available, long flowering season
Phlomis russeliana	1.0 (39")	0.6 (2)	golden yellow, plus good seed heads	E, large, ground-covering	ESu	S, LSh		5	very good weed-suppressing ground cover; always looks good
Phlox paniculata	1.2 (4)	0.4 (16")	pink, violet, magenta, white, fragrant	upright habit	MSu–LSu	S, LSh		4	very variable in vigour, at best long-lived
Phygelius species	1.2 (4)	1.0 (39")	red, pink, yellow	dark leaves, untidy semi-shrubby habit	MSu–LSu	S		8	often grown either as a wall shrub or treated as herbaceous
Polygonatum species	0.3-1.5 (12"–5')	0.4 (16")	white, yellowish	very elegant, arching stems	MSu–LSu	LSh–Sh		3-6	varied group, with wide size range
Primula elatior; P. vulgaris and polyanthus varieties	0.2 (8")	0.3 (12")	yellow; hybrids red, pink, blue, brown	rosettes of ground-hugging leaves	Win–Spr	LSh–Sh		5	very popular plants that can be long-lived; more or less summer dormant so can be squeezed in among other plants
Primula florindae	0.2–0.8 (8"–32")	0.4 (16")	yellow, orange, spicy scent	low rosettes	MSu	S, LSh	M	6	the most long-lived of many moisture-loving Asian primulas
Pulmonaria species (some)	0.4 (16")	0.4 (16")	pink, pale blue	large leaves, low, some with silver markings	Spr	LSh–Sh		3-6	long flowering season, leaves deteriorate in dry summers
Pulsatilla vulgaris	0.4 (16")	0.3 (12")	violet, red, white	ferny, tight clump	Spr, MSu	S	D	5	Fluffy seed heads; hates being transplanted
Rodgersia – many varieties	0.6/1.0 (2'/39")	1.0 (39")	white, pink heads of small flowers	very large, often bronze-tinged	Spr–Aut	LSh	M, Ø	6	foliage is main feature; easily scorched if too dry
Rudbeckia fulgida	0.3/0.8 (12/32")	0.5 (20")	dark-centred yellow daisies	dark, low level	LSu–Aut	S		4	long-flowering, reliable, slowly spreading
Salvia microphylla	1.2 (4)	0.9 (3)	red, pink, white	small, aromatic, bushy shape	LSu–Aut	S		8	really a shrub, but best hard pruned in spring; variable – many varieties

Nepeta x *faassenii*

Phygelius x *rectus* 'African Queen'

Polygonatum curvistylum

Primula elatior

Salvia x *jamensis* 'Hot Lips'

NAME	DESCRIPTION					CULTIVATION			NOTES
	HEIGHT M (FT)	SPREAD M (FT)	FLOWERS/FRUIT	FOLIAGE	SEASON OF INTEREST	LIGHT	OTHER	HARD -INESS	
PERENNIALS									
Salvia nemorosa, *S. x superba*, *S. x sylvestris* varieties	0.7 (27")	0.4 (16")	purple, violet, pink, blue	aromatic, tight clumps	ESu	S	D	5	can repeat flower if cut back after first flush
Sanguisorba species	0.6/1.5 (2/5)	0.6 (2)	dark red, pink, usually in bobbles	divided, elegant	MSu–LSu	S	(M)	4	very good foliage from spring on; can flop badly when in flower
Satureja montana	0.8 (32")	0.3 (12")	small lilac spikes	small, aromatic	ESu	S	D	4	often used as a culinary herb
Saxifrage fortunei varieties	0.3 (12")	0.3 (12")	white, red, pink	large, decorative	Aut	LSh–Sh	Ø	6	wide range of varieties increasingly available
Sedum spectabile, *S. telephium* varieties	0.6 (2)	0.6 (2)	pink, seed heads persistent through winter	fleshy, grey-green	LSu–Aut	S	D	6	slowly form clumps, but not spreading
Selinum wallichianum	1.0 (39")	0.8 (32")	white 'cow parsley' heads	very fine, almost filigree	MSu–LSu	S, LSh		7	long-lived plant for foliage and subtle flower colour
Symphytum × uplandicum 'Axminster Gold'	0.5 (20")	0.6 (2)	purple	wide yellow-variegated leaves, low clump	Spr–Aut	S–Sh		5	one of the few comfrey species that does not spread aggressively
Thalictrum species	1.5 (5)	0.3 (12")	purple, white	very divided, graceful	ESu	S, LSh	M	6	elegant plants, some flower later in summer
Tricyrtis species	0.3–0.9 (12"–3')	0.4 (16")	pink, white, spotted	broad leaves, upright stems	LSu–Aut	LSh		5	elegant plants, can be slow to establish
Verbacscum nigrum	0.3–1.2 (12"–4')	0.4 (16")	yellow in narrow spike, good seed heads	basal rosette in first year	MSu	S	D	5	biennial, will usually seed after flowering
Verbena bonariensis	1.5 (5)	0.2 (8")	deep violet heads	sparse, almost all stem	MSu–Aut	S	D	7	very long-flowering; very short-lived but usually self-sows
Veronicastrum varieties	2.0 (7)	0.5 (20")	purple, blue, pink, in narrow spikes	very elegant upright stems	MSu	S		3	long-lived and good for winter structure
Vinca minor	0.3 (12")	1.0 (39")	blue, purple, pink	E, small, on stems which root as they go	Spr	LSh–Sh		4	many different varieties; useful and vigorous ground cover
Viola cornuta	0.3 (12")	0.4 (16")	violet, purple, pink	light green spreading tufts	Spr	LSh–Sh		7	useful to let run between other plants
GRASSES									
Bouteloua gracilis	0.6 (2)	0.3 (12")	maroon, very distinctive heads	bluish	Aut	S		4	can be used as a rough lawn substitute
Briza media	0.7 (27")	0.2 (8")	large, distinctive heads	low tight clumps	MSu	S		4	untidy after flowering

Sedum 'Matrona'

Tricyrtis 'Shimone'

Sanguisorba officinalis

Vinca minor

Bouteloua gracilis

GRASSES

NAME	DESCRIPTION					CULTIVATION			NOTES
	HEIGHT M (FT)	SPREAD M (FT)	FLOWERS/FRUIT	FOLIAGE	SEASON OF INTEREST	LIGHT	OTHER	HARD-INESS	
Calamagrostis x *acutiflora* 'Overdam'	1.0 (39")	0.4 (16")	fawn heads	leaves slightly variegated, very upright growth habit	ESu–Win	S		4	exceptionally good grass for vertical accents
Calamagrostis brachytricha (*Achnatherum brachytricha*)	1.2 (4)	0.3 (12")	mauvish, narrow heads	upright	LSu–Aut	S		4	can seed aggressively
Carex: e.g. *C. comans*, *C. flagellifera*, and *C. testacea*	0.4 (16")	0.3 (12")	inconspicuous	E, these species have bronze or brown foliage	All	S, LSh		7	extremely good all-year plants; many other *Carex* (sedges) species
Chionochloa conspicua	0.6/1.8 (2/6)	0.9 (3)	open panicles on arching stems	tight tufts of coarse leaves	Aut	S		8	a smaller version of the well-known pampas grass
Festuca glauca	0.15/0.4 (6"/16")	0.2 (8")	straw-coloured	E, blue-grey, fine	All	S	D	4	popular dwarf grass, a useful filler
Hakonechloa macra	0.6 (2)	0.6 (2)	inconspicuous	fresh green, tidy 'combed' look	ESu–Aut	S, LSh		6	very elegant; variegated form 'Aureola' also popular
Helictotrichon sempervirens	0.4/0.9 (16"/36")	0.6 (2)	straw-coloured, slender	blue-grey	ESu–Aut	S	D	4	best appreciated if not crowded by other plants
Imperata cylindrica	0.6 (2)	0.3 (12")	silvery panicles	blood-red colour	ESu–Aut	S		8	can perform badly in cool climates and may be invasive in warm ones
Koeleria glauca	0.6 (2)	0.3 (12")	inconspicuous	grey-blue	ESu–Aut	S		6	can be short-lived, but often self-sows
Miscanthus sinensis – dwarf varieties	1.0 (39")	0.8 (32")	reed-like panicles held above foliage	dark, neatly tufted	LSu–Win	S, LSh		5	most varieties are large, so important to get the size right; spreads slowly
Molinia caerulea (not *arundinacea* varieties)	0.8 (32")	0.3 (12")	stiff, dark flower heads	tight tufts with upright habit; good autumn colour	MSu–Aut	S		4	tussock forming, can seed strongly; good on poor acid soils
Panicum virgatum, smaller varieties	1.2 (4)	0.8 (32")	very fine flower/seed heads in cloud-like masses	often turning red or orange in autumn	LSu–Win	S		4	some varieties very large, so choose carefully; can be late to emerge in spring
Pennisetum alopecuroides varieties	0.5–1.4 (20"–4')	0.6 (2)	very fluffy foxtail-shaped heads	moderately tight tufts	LSu–Win	S		5	not always easy, but very rewarding
Schizachyrium scoparium	1.2 (4)	0.4 (16")	variety of russet colours	green, can be bluish, reddish in autumn	Aut–Win	S		3	can flop badly, sometimes short-lived

Calamagrostis brachytricha

Carex tenuiculmis 'Cappuccino'

Hakonechloa macra

Miscanthus sinensis 'Zebrinus'

Miscanthus sinensis 'Yakushima Dwarf'

NAME	DESCRIPTION					CULTIVATION			NOTES
	HEIGHT M (FT)	SPREAD M (FT)	FLOWERS/FRUIT	FOLIAGE	SEASON OF INTEREST	LIGHT	OTHER	HARD -INESS	
GRASSES									
Sesleria species	0.2/0.4 (8"/ 16")	0.3 (12")	white, not very showy	fresh green slowly spreading mats	Spr–Aut	S	D	4	good on poor soils; foliage colour complements other colours nicely
Sporobolus heterolepis	0.6/1.2 (2/4)	0.6 (2)	very fine, aromatic	fine, dense tufts	LSu–Win	S	D	4	potentially very good, but slow to establish
Stipa calamagrostis	0.9 (3)	0.3 (12")	fawn	dark, narrow	LSu–Aut	S		5	tends to flop
Stipa gigantea	0.6/2.0 (2/7)	0.7 (27")	oat-like, very airy	E, dense tufts	ESu–Aut	S		5	sounds large, but heads are 'transparent'
Stipa tenuissima (*Nassella tenuissima*)	0.5 (20")	0.2 (8")	very light, fluffy heads	extremely fine leaves, tight tufts	MSu–Win	S	D	7	can be short-lived, but nearly always self-sows
Uncinia rubra	0.3 (12")	0.4 (16")	inconspicuous	E, red-brown, low-growing	All	S, LSh	(M)	8	good low-level interest
CLIMBERS									
Clematis alpina C.macropetala varieties	2.5 (8)	0.6 (2)	blue, purple or pink	divided	Spr	S, LSh		3	can be combined with taller climbers
Clematis: compact patio varieties	1.5 (5)	0.3 (12")	big, showy, wide range of colours	mostly green, divided	ESu–Aut	S, LSh		5	ideal for small spaces or container growing
Clematis orientalis	8.0 (26)	1.0 (39")	yellow, 'lemon-peel'; fluffy winter seed heads	very small	MSu–Aut	S, LSh		5	can grow very large but may be pruned much smaller
Hedera species	15.0 (50)	12.0 (39+)*	inconspicuous	E, wide range of colours and variegation	All	S–Sh		5	growth*, including spread as ground cover, can be very vigorous needing ruthless control; variegated varieties less so
Jasminum species	3.0 (10)	0.8 (32")	white or yellow; usually fragrant	small leaves, dense	Spr	S, LSh		6-7	may need tying to supports and training
Lonicera periclymenum	3.5 (12)	0.4 (16")	white, yellow, fragrant	slightly grey	ESu–MSu	S, LSh		4	twining climber; most orange/red forms are not scented
Parthenocissus species	12.0 (39)	0.1 (4")	inconspicuous	lobed; spectacular autumn colour	Aut	S, LSh		4	self-clinging, ideal as decorative cladding for buildings; too vigorous for fences/garden walls
Schisandra species	10.0 (33)	0.4 (16")	cream, fragrant; red berries	medium-sized	MSu	S		4	fruit edible, but both male and female plants needed
Trachelospermum asiaticum	6.0 (20)	0.4 (16")	cream, very fragrant	E, glossy	MSu	S		8	*T. jasminoides* similar but less hardy

Jasminum nudiflorum

Clematis 'Hagley Hybrid'

Parthenocissus henryana

Parthenocissus quinquefolia

Trachelospermum jasminoides

NAME	DESCRIPTION					CULTIVATION			NOTES
	HEIGHT M (FT)	SPREAD M (FT)	FLOWERS/FRUIT	FOLIAGE	SEASON OF INTEREST	LIGHT	OTHER	HARD -INESS	
BULBS									
Allium – 'drumstick' varieties	1.0 (39")	0.15 (6")	purple shades	dies rapidly after flowering	ESu	S		4	dramatic 'balls on sticks' look, good summer seed heads; can self-seed, but persistence not guaranteed
Allium – smaller varieties	0.20 (8")	0.07 (3")	various	dies rapidly after flowering	Spr–ESu	S (some LSh)		4	.any good for very shallow soils, e.g. green roofs; some can self-seed and become weedy
Chionodoxa species	0.12 (5")	0.07 (3")	blue	fine, little impact	Spr	S, LSh		4	very easy early spring bulb
Corydalis flexuosa	0.15 (6")	0.1 (4")	intense blue	divided, non-linear	Spr	LSh		5	spreads slowly
Corydalis solida	0.15 (6")	0.1 (4")	pink, red	divided, non-linear	Spr	S, LSh		5	can self-seed, but usually limited
Crocus species	0.12 (5")	0.05 (2")	yellow, white, purple	fine, little impact	Spr	S, LSh		4	many different varieties; early; vulnerable to rodents
Galanthus species	0.15 (6")	0.05 (2")	white	fine, clump forming	Spr	S, LSh		3-4	very early, very perennial – more every year!
Muscari species	0.15 (6")	0.05 (2")	blue, purple	fine, clump forming	Spr	S		4	usually increase well year to year
Narcissus – smaller varieties	up to 0.30 (12")	0.15 (6")	yellow, white	broad linear, long-lasting	Spr	S, LSh		3-4	persistent post-flowering leaves can be untidy but must not be cut; usually increase well year on year
	There is a bewildering array of daffodil varieties, most of which are more than 30cm (12in) high. Increasing numbers of smaller varieties are available, eg, 'Tête-à-tête'. 'Cyclamineus' types are particularly good as they flower early and are small. 'Jonquil' and 'Tazetta' types are scented. Tazettas are not so hardy, and need a warm site.								
Scilla species	0.15 (6")	0.05 (2")	blue	fine, clump forming	Spr	S, LSh		4	usually increase well year to year
Tulipa – smaller varieties	0.15–0.4 (6"–16")	0.05 (2")	anything but blue	broad, not attractive	Spr	S		4	cannot be relied on to flower again year after year
	There is a huge number of tulip varieties. 'Species' types tend to be small, informal and (sometimes) have more perennial qualities, but need full sun and fertile soil. 'Kaufmanniana' types flower early and are dwarf; 'Darwin' types are tall, stiff-stemmed and often re-flower well.								

Allium schoenoprasum

Chionodoxa

Corydalis solida subsp solida 'Beth Evans'

Galanthus elwesii 'Comet'

Muscari armeniacum

Designers' and garden contacts

We made use of the work of the following garden designers in this book, either photographing gardens they had made specifically for this project, interviewing them or making extensive use of small gardens they have designed.

Gardens of Appeltern
www.appeltern.nl

Carolien Barkman
www.carolienbarkman.nl

Joanne Bernstein
www.joannebernstein-gardendesign.com

Robert Broekema
www.robertbroekema.nl

Luc Engelhard
www.lucengelhard.nl

Leen Goedegebuure
www.kijktuinen.nl

Annie Guilfoyle
www.creative-landscapes.com

Frank Heijligers & Frank van der Linden
www.wijzijnvannature.nl

Jacqueline van der Kloet
www.theetuin.nl

Carrie Preston
www.studiotoop.nl

Erwin Stam
www.erwinstam-tuinstudio.com

Ruud Vermeer
www.meneervermeertuinen.nl

Spencer Viner
www.northeleven.co.uk

Cleve West
www.clevewest.com

Carol Whitehead
www.carolwhitehead.co.uk

Joost Willems and Jan van Opstal
www.heerenhof.be

Tom de Witte and Corinne Lecluyse
www.tomdewitte.nl

The following gardens are open on a regular basis:

Gardens of Appeltern
www.appeltern.nl

de Heerenhof
Maastricht, South Limburg, Netherlands
www.heerenhof.be

Kijktuinen Nunspeet
www.kijktuinen.nl

the Theetuin
Weesp – near Amsterdam, Netherlands
www.theetuin.nl

The London gardens listed below are open to the public under the charitable National Gardens Scheme, on specific days only, often only on one day each year. Details of the opening days, times, and full addresses can be found at www.ngs.org.uk

Joanne Bernstein, Mercers Road

Paul Cox, Alexandra Park Road Gardens

Clare Dryhurst, Cornflower Terrace

Zaki & Ruth Elia, Hillfield Park

Spencer Viner, Brownlow Road

Index

Page numbers in *italic* indicate a caption to an illustration. Page numbers in **bold** indicate a boxed entry. Case Studies and Masterclasses also have their own headings.

A

Abelia **85**
 A. x *grandiflora* **188**
  A. g. 'Francis Mason' *188*
Abies koreana 'Silberlocke' **95**
Abutilon **85**, *113*, **188**
Acaena **71**, **95**
Acanthus **69**, **89**
 A. spinosus *98*, *99*, **193**
Acer (maple) *45*
 A. campestre **89**
 A. griseum **89**, *188*
 A. palmatum (Japanese maple) *79*, **89**, *92*, *166*, **188**
  A. p. 'Osakazuki' *45*, *188*
 A. pensylvanicum *49*
Achillea *55*, **70**, **82**, **95**, *99*, *166*, **193**
 A. 'Feuerland' *193*
 A. filipendulina 'Parker's Variety' *128*
 A. millefolium *129*
 A. 'Mondpagode' *107*
Achnatherum brachytricha see *Calamagrostis brachytricha*
acid soil *16*
 plants for **17**, **177**
Acorus **101**
 A. gramineus **17**
Actaea **87**
 A. racemosa **92**
Actinidia
 A. chinensis (kiwi fruit) **117**, **177**, *180*
 A. kolomikta **93**
Agapanthus **89**, *99*, *166*, **193**
 A. inapertus **85**
Agastache **166**
 A. rugosa **87**, *99*, **193**
agaves *105*
Ageratina altissima **85**
Ajuga **71**, **92**, **95**, **193**
 A. reptans 'Catlin's Giant' *193*
Akebia quinata **117**
Albizia julibrissin *166*, *188*, **188**
Alcea (hollyhock) **57**, **98**, **130**
Alchemilla **69**
 A. mollis **17**, *43*, *54*, *75*, *99*, *166*
alkaline soil *16*, *16*
 plants for **17**
Alkema, Willy and Jan *51*
Allium **17**, *59*, **87**, *124*, *140*, **201**
 A. cristophii *66*
 A. giganteum *98*
 A. hollandicum *14*
 A. schoenoprasum (chives) *133*, *157*, *185*, **201**
 A. ursinum *131*
 drumstick varieties **201**
Aloysia citrodora *103*, **188**
alpine strawberries **177**
alpines *118*, *144*
Alton Infant School *133*
Amaranthus **87**, **130**
Amelanchier **17**, **89**, *130*, *135*, **144**, **188**

A. canadensis **86**
A. lamarckii *189*
Amiel, Wayne *105*
Amsonia **70**, **86**, **89**, **193**
Anagallis arvensis (scarlet pimpernel) **131**
Anaphalis **82**, **93**, **193**
 A. triplinervis *193*
Anemone
 A. blanda **68**, *157*
 A. nemorosa **68**
Angelica **70**
annuals *56–7*
 for containers *161*
 fast growing *105*
 long-flowering **82**
 seasonal performances **80**
 for seed heads **87**
 soil for *16*
 winter *57*
Antennaria dioica **158**
Anthemis
 A. punctata subsp *cupaniana* **93**, **193**
Appeltern see Gardens of Appeltern
apples **176**, *176*, *185*
 see also *Malus*
apricots **176**
 see also *Prunus*
aquatics **131**
Aquilegia *55*, **70**, *81*
Aralia elata *11*, *45*, **96**, *99*, **189**
Arbutus unedo (strawberry tree) *74*
Armeria **17**, **95**
Aronia **89**, *130*, **144**, **189**
Arrowsmith, Chris *143*
Artemisia
 A. abrotanum **103**, *192*, **192**
 A. pontica *53*
 A. stelleriana **93**, **193**
Arum italicum **89**
 A. i. 'Pictum' *86*, **193**
Aruncus dioicus **129**, **144**
 A. d. 'Kneiffii' **89**, **193**
Arundo donax var *versicolor* **93**
Asclepias **129**
aspect of garden *11–12*, *14*
 for climbers *114*
 for vegetables *180*
Aster **70**, **144**
 A. divaricatus **85**, **194**
 A. dumosus **85**
 A. ericoides **85**
 A. x *frickartii* **194**
  A. x *f.* 'Mönch' *43*, **82**, *82*, **194**
 A. lateriflorus **129**
 A. pyrenaeus **82**
 A. thomsonii 'Nanus' **82**
 see also *Symphyotrichum*
Astilbe **17**, *54*, **68**, **92**, *99*, *166*, **194**
 A. rivularis **89**
Astilboides tabularis *81*
Astrantia **69**, *81*
 A. major **82**, **194**

A. m. 'Sunningdale Variegated' **93**
A. 'Roma' **194**
Athyrium filix-femina *79*
Atriplex halimus **93**, **189**
aubergines **175**
aubretia *118*
autumn foliage *86*, *89*, *111*
azalea see *Rhododendron*

B

Baccharis **95**
 B. patagonica **189**
balcony *38*
Ballota pseudodictamnus **93**, **192**
bamboos *36*, **50**
banana see *Musa basjoo*
Baptisia australis *99*
bare legs syndrome *85*
bark effects **89**
Barkman, Carolien *11*, *23*, *27*, *28*, *81*, *123*, *133*
beans **174**
Beardshaw, Chris *79*
bedding plants *56*
beech see *Fagus*
beetroot *157*, **178**, *180*
Begonia *57*
bell jar *183*
Bellis perennis (lawn daisy) **131**
Berberis
 B. darwinii **95**
 B. linearifolia **95**
 B. microphylla **95**
 B. thunbergii **89**, **92**, **189**
  B. t. f. *atropurpurea* **50**
  B. t. f. *atropurpurea* 'Harlequin' *50*
Bergenia *55*, **71**, **95**, *99*, *118*, **194**
Bernstein, Joanne *21*, *37*, **106–7**
berries *86*, **87**, *130*
Betula (birch) *45*, *130*
 B. nana *166*, **189**
biennials *57*
 seasonal performances **86**
 for seed heads **87**
biodiversity, plants for **128**
birch see *Betula*
Blaauwboer, Marianne *23*
blackberries *177*
blackcurrants **177**
Blechnum chilense **89**
Bloemsma, Fokke *158*
bluebell *65*
blueberries **177**
bog plants *127*, **131**
Boston ivy see *Parthenocissus*
boundaries *12*, *25*
Bouteloua gracilis *101*, *198*, **198**
Bouwhuysen, Kristof Van Den *13*
box see *Buxus*
brassicas **174**, *175*
Brekelmans, Tom *79*
Bremness, Lesley *142*
bricks for paths *147*, *148*, *150*

Briza
 B. maxima **87**
 B. media *98*, **101**, **198**
broad beans *180*
Broekema, Robert *11*, *21*, *25*, *30*, *61*
Broussonetia papyrifera *81*
Brunnera macrophylla *54*, **93**, **194**
 B. m. 'Dawson's White' *194*
Buddleja davidii **85**, **103**, **189**
 B. d. 'Nanho Blue' *189*
bulbs *58–9*, **201**
 narrow **70**
 seasonal performances **80**
 for seed heads **87**
 spring-flowering **68**
 for tropical look *105*
Bupleurum fruticosum **95**, **189**
bush fruit **177**
Butomus umbellatus **131**
Buxus (box) *46*, *48*, **50**, *51*, *65*, *81*, **95**
 B. sempervirens **50**, *99*, *166*, **189**

C

cacti *105*
Calamagrostis
 C. x *acutiflora*
  C. x *a.* 'Karl Foerster' **70**, *98*, *99*, **101**, *199*
 C. x *acutiflora*
  C. x *a.* 'Overdam' **93**, *99*, **101**, *101*
 C. brachytricha *43*, *99*, **101**, *199*, **199**
Calamintha **69**, *166*
 C. nepeta *30*
  C. n. 'Blue Cloud' *101*
Calendula officinalis (marigold) *27*, *57*, **129**, *133*
callaloo **174**
Callicarpa bodinieri **87**
Calluna **17**
 C. vulgaris **92**, *192*
Caltha palustris **17**, **131**
Camellia **17**, *45*, *166*
Campanula **17**
 C. cochleariifolia **158**
 C. portenschlagiana **71**
 C. poscharskyana *55*, **71**
 dwarf **158**
cane fruit **177**
Canna *105*, *105*, *169*
capsicum **175**
Carex (sedge) *55*, **93**, *101*, *101*, *118*, *157*
 C. comans *59*, **92**, *98*, **199**
 C. elata 'Aurea' **92**
 C. flagellifera **92**, **199**
 C. morrowii 'Variegata' *79*
 C. oshimensis 'Evergold' *169*
 C. tenuiculmis 'Cappuccino' *199*
 C. testacea **92**, **199**
Carpinus betulus (hornbeam) *21*, *48*, *49*, **50**, *51*
carrots **178**

Carya **49**
Case Studies
  compact productive plot
    184–5
  design tricks **38–9**
  plant layering in a small
    garden **72–5**
  plant-packed small garden
    106–7
  potted front garden **168–9**
  suburban wildlife retreat
    134–5
castor oil plant see *Ricinus*
  communis
Catalpa **49**
  C. bignonioides 49
  C. b. 'Aurea' **92**, *188*, **188**
catmint see *Nepeta*
Ceanothus **17**, **95**, 113, 114, **189**
  C. 'A.T. Johnson' **85**
  C. 'Autumnal Blue' **85**
  C. 'Burkwoodii' **85**
  C. impressus **85**
celery 175
Centaurea (cornflower) **69**, 130
  C. cyanus 56
  C. montana 69
  C. scabiosa 129
Centranthus ruber 81, 166, **194**
Ceratostigma 89, **194**
  C. plumbaginoides 194
Cercis **49**
  C. canadensis 'Forest
    Pansy' **92**, 188
Chamaecyparis lawsoniana 95
chamomile *147*
Chasmanthium latifolium 130
Chelone **85**, 144, **194**
Chenopodium (fat hen) 131
cherries 176
cherry, ornamental
  see *Prunus cerasifera*
chillis 175
Chinese garden 30, 36, 79
Chionochloa conspicua
  99, 101, *199*
Chionodoxa 59, **68**, 201, *201*
chives see *Allium*
  schoenoprasum
Choisya **95**
  C. ternata 'Sundance' **73**
Chrysanthemum 85, **194**
Cijsouw, Joke and Henk 7
Cistus **17**, **71**, 93, 103, **192**
Clematis 112, *112*, 114, 118, 166
  C. alpina **200**
  C. armandii **95**, 114, **117**, *117*
  C. 'Bill MacKenzie' **86**, **87**, *87*
  C. 'Hagley Hybrid' **200**
  C. macropetala **200**
  C. montana 111
  C. orientalis 130, **200**
  C. recta 'Purpurea' *103*
  for patios **200**
Cleome 56
Clerodendrum 43
  C. trichotomum 34
climbers 23, 35, 36, 53, 62,
  110–17, **200**
  for colourful foliage **93**
  in containers **117**, 166
  as dividers 115
  evergreen 94, **95**
  for foliage 116–17
  positioning 114–15
  seasonal performances **86**
  for seed heads **87**
  self-clinging **112**
  tendril **112**
  thorny **113**
  twining **113**

clover see *Trifolium*
cob **151**
Colchicum 59
colour **27**
  containers *155*
  for focus 33
  green 31
  walls 27
  see also under foliage
compost 16, 133
  for containers 162
  green root substrates 163
  home-produced 163
  peat-based **163**
  peat-free **163**
  soil-based **163**
concrete alternatives **151**
conifers 94, **95**
containers **11**, 31, 35, 152–69
  for annuals 56
  choosing plants for 156–9
  climbers for **117**, 166
  flexibility 73
  maintenance 162–5
  moving around 162
  perennials for **166**
  shallow **158**
  shapes **158**
  shrubs for **166**
  trees for **166**
  types 156–7
  vegetables for *157*, 180, *183*
Convallaria majalis 103, 166,
  194, *194*
Convolvulus cneorum 93, 166,
  192
coppicing **48**
  trees and shrubs for **49**
cordons 176
Cordyline australis 166
  C. a. 'Red Star' **73**
coriander 180
cornflower see *Centaurea*
  cyanus
Cornus (dogwood) 45
  C. alba 49
    C. a. 'Sibirica' *49*
  C. alternifolia 96
    C. a. 'Argentea' *93*, **189**
  C. controversa **96**
  C. kousa 'Milky Way' *14*
  C. sanguinea 49, **144**
  C. stolonifera 49
Corokia cotoneaster 166
Coronilla valentina subsp
  glauca *93*, **189**
corridors for wildlife 124–5
Corydalis **68**
  C. flexuosa **201**
  C. solida **201**
    C. s. subsp *solida*
    'Beth Evans' *201*
Corylus (hazel) **48**, 49
  C. avellana **144**
  C. maxima 'Purpurea' **92**, **189**
Cosmos 56
Cotinus coggygria (smoke
  bush) **49**, 89
  C. c. 'Royal Purple' *81*, 90,
    92, **189**
Cotoneaster **87**, 95, 113, 129,
  130, **189**
  C. franchetii **50**
  C. horizontalis 113
  C. x suecicus 'Coral Beauty'
    189
cottage gardens 66
Cotula **95**
coulisses 22
courgettes 175
Cox, Paul 33

crab apples see *Malus*
Crataegus (hawthorn) **87**, 130,
  188
  C. 'Autumn Glory' **89**
  C. monogyna 89
crazy paving 150, *151*
creeping plants 62, 94
Crocosmia 70, 85, **99**
  C. 'Lucifer' 105
Crocus 59, **68**, **201**
Cryptomeria japonica
  'Vilmoriniana' **95**
cucumbers 175
Cund, David 168–9
Cyclamen
  C. coum 68
  C. hederifolium 59
Cynara cardunculus 89, **96**,
  99, **194**
Cytisus 166, **192**
  C. scoparius 192

D
daffodil see *Narcissus*
Dahlia 82, 105, *165*, *169*, **194**
  D. 'Nathalie's Wedding' 82
daisy, lawn see *Bellis perennis*
damsons 176
Daphne 103, 166, **189**
  D. mezereum 189
Darmera peltata 89, *99*, **194**
Davies, Teresa 35
Day, Elsa 31
decking 30, 33, **38**, *147*, *148*, 150
Delphinium 98
Deschampsia cespitosa
  17, **69**, *107*
design tricks 18–39
detail 31
diagonal lines 26
Dianthus **17**, 103, 166, **194**
Diascia 82, **195**
Dicentra 89, **195**
Dicksonia antarctica (tree
  fern) 79
Dierama 96, **99**, **195**
Digitalis (foxglove) *7*, 57, **70**,
  99, **195**
  D. ferruginea **87**, 195
  D. x mertonensis 79
dill **180**
Dillon, Helen 14
Dipsacus fullonum **87**, 130
disease resistance 179
dogwood see *Cornus*
doors to garden 37, *37*
drainage 16, 141
  plants for poorly drained soil **17**
Dregea sinensis **95**
driveways 147
drought-tolerant plants 140
dry soil 16
  plants for **17**
  due to trees 44, 45
dummy doors 21
Dunnett, Nigel 139, 142, 143

E
east-facing garden 14
eating outdoors 11–12, 21, 37
Echinacea **69**, 70, 87, 129, 166
  E. pallida **144**
  E. purpurea 55, **82**, **99**, 130, **195**
    E. p. 'Magnus' *128*
Echinops **96**, 130
  E. ritro 74
ecofriendly gardens 136–57
Edwards, Sabina *157*
Elaeagnus
  E. x ebbingei **92**, **189**, *189*
  E. pungens **92**, 103, **189**

elder see *Sambucus*
Elia, Zaki and Ruth 11, 25, 31, *118*
energy consumption
  assessment 148
Engelhard, Luc 21, 25, 27
Enkianthus 89, **189**
Epimedium 55, **68**, **95**, 98, 99,
  166, **195**
  E. x perralchicum
    'Fröhnleiten' *185*
  E. x youngianum 'Niveum'
    195
Equisetum hyemale 131
Erica (heather) **17**, **71**, 166, **192**
Erinus alpinus **95**
Eryngium **87**, **96**
  E. bourgatii **17**, **195**
  E. giganteum 57, *107*
Erysimum (wallflower) **57**
  dwarf 118
  E. 'Bowles's Mauve' **195**, *195*
Escallonia **85**, **189**
Eschscholzia californica 57
espaliers 176
Eucalyptus **49**, 166, **188**
Euonymus
  E. europaeus 130
  E. fortunei **50**, 92, 93, 166, **189**
  E. japonicus 92, 93, 166, **189**
Eupatorium 54, 129, **144**
Euphorbia **69**
  E. amygdaloides
    var *robbiae* **95**, **195**
  E. characias **17**, **95**, **99**, **195**
    E. c. subsp. *wulfenii* **73**, 195
  E. cyparissias **17**, **55**, 59
    69
  E. epithymoides 187
  E. mellifera 79, 103, **190**
  E. peplus (petty spurge) 131
  E. polychroma 54, **69**
Eurybia x herveyi **85**
evening primrose
  see *Oenothera*
evergreens 80, 94–5
exotic planting 25, 104–5
  in containers 162

F
F₁ hybrids 179
Fagus sylvatica (beech) **48**, **50**
  hedges 118
fat hen see *Chenopodium*
Fatsia japonica 96, **144**
feeding plants in containers
  165
fences 13, 22, 111, 135, 150
  aspect 114
ferns 30, 45, **68**, 79, 81, *118*
  tree ferns 79, 105
fertilisers **165**
Festuca 101
  F. glauca 93, **199**
Fibigia clypeata **87**
Ficus (fig)
  F. afghanistanica 185
  F. carica 105, *166*, *167*
fig see *Ficus*
Filipendula **17**, **144**
  F. ulmaria 129
Florence fennel 174
flower heads 80
  seasonal performances **86**
focal points 32–3, *37*
  vertical 34
foliage effects *38*, **80**, 88–93,
  160–1
  climbers 116–17
  colour **50**, 90–3
  grasses 101
  purple/dark **92**

scented leaves **103**
seasonal performances **86**
silver/grey **93**
variegated 90–1
yellow/gold **92**
food chains 123
forage crops **175**
forget-me-not
  see Myosotis sylvatica
Fothergilla **89**, **190**
foxglove *see Digitalis*
Frankel, Hermione *31*
French beans *174*
frogs *127, 127*
Frost, Adam *111*
frost protection 183
fruit 170–85, **176–7**
  requirements 180–1
  soil for 16
Fuchsia 166
  F. 'Golden Treasure' **92**
  F. magellanica 46, **190**
    F. m. var. *gracilis* 190
functions of garden 11–12
furniture, garden 150

G

gabions *151, 151*
Galanthus (snowdrop) *27, 59,*
  68, **201**
  G. elwesii 'Comet' *201*
Galega orientalis *14*
Gardens of Appeltern *14, 34,*
  43, 45, 49, 61, 96, 115, 155,
  161, 180
garlic *175*
Garrya elliptica **113**
Gaura lindheimeri 81
Geranium 43, 54, 65, 69, 81, **89**,
  144, *166*
  G. 'Anne Thomson' *21*
  G. x *cantabrigiense*
    'Cambridge' **195**
  G. endressii **69**, **82**, 98, 99, **195**
  G. x *magnificum* **195**
  G. x *oxonianum* 82, **195**
  G. pratense **69**, 98, *98*
  G. procurrens **85**
  G. sanguineum **17**, **69**
  G. soboliferum **89**
  G. sylvaticum **70**
Geum triflorum **87**, **98**
Gielen, Annelies *135*
Gillenia trifoliata **89**, **195**
Gladiolus 59
Gleditsia triacanthos **48**
globe artichokes *175*
Goedegebuure, Leen *33, 49, 96*
Golding, Sally **168–9**
Goldsmith, Neil *157*
gooseberries **177**
Gould, Kate *23*, *147*
granite setts 38, *139*, *147*
grass mesh *147*
grasses, ornamental *11*, 29,
  36, 55, **65**, **69**, **70**, 81, 100–2,
  106–7, *140*, **198–200**
  autumn colour **89**
  big airy **101**
  for colourful foliage **92–3**
  for containers **161**, *169*
  medium-sized structural **101**
  seasonal performances 80, **86**
  small with good leaves **101**
  small with good seed heads
    101
  see also specific grasses
grassland 66
gravel *75*, *143*, *147*
green walls 118

Griselinia littoralis 'Dixon's
  Cream' **92**
ground-hugging plants 71
Guilfoyle, Annie *21, 25, 26, 33,*
  35, 35, **38–9**, *79, 81*
Guinness, Bunny *173*
Gunning, Lydia *23*

H

Habet, Nada *155*
Hadlow College *144*
Hakonechloa macra 21, 33, **99**,
  101, *199*, **199**
  H. m. 'Aureola' **92**
half-hardy plants 56
Hall, Marney *133*
Hallam, Adrian *143*
Hamamelis mollis **103**, **190**
  H. m. var *pallida* **190**
hard landscaping using eco-
  friendly materials 139, 141,
  147, 150–1
Hawkins, Samantha *35*
hay meadow 66
hazel *see Corylus*
heather *see Erica*
Hebe **71**, **85**, **95**, **99**, *166*, **192**
  H. albicans 53
  H. cupressoides 94, **95**, **192**
  H. ochracea 'James Stirling' **92**
  H. 'Pewter Dome' **93**
  H. 'Pink Pixie' **192**
  H. 'Red Edge' **93**
Hedera (ivy) 45, 94, **112**, 117,
  118, *118*, *157*, *166*, **200**
  H. helix **95**, **129**, *130*
  H. hibernica **95**
hedges 22, *38*, **38**, 43, 50, *118*
Heerenhof, De *11*, *61*
Helenium 70
  H. 'Moerheim Beauty' *107*
Helianthemum **71**, 118
Helianthus *130*
Helichrysum
  H. italicum
    H. i. subsp *serotinum* **192**
  H. petiolare 93
Helictotrichon sempervirens
  93, *199*
Heliotropium **82**
Helleborus 55, **68**, **95**
  H. foetidus 89
  H. x *hybridus* **99**, *166*, **196**, *196*
Hemerocallis **17**, 69, 74, **99**, **196**
herbs *174*, **175**
heritage vegetables *179*
Hesperantha coccinea 85, **196**
Heuchera **68**, 92, **95**, 118, *166*, **196**
  H. villosa 'Palace Purple' *169*
Heydon, Luke *157*
Hibiscus syriacus **190**
  H. s. 'Coelestis' **85**
Higgins, Rita *139*
Hof Ter Dieren *30*
Holboellia coriacea **95**
holly *see Ilex*
hollyhock *see Alcea*
honeysuckle *see Lonicera*
Hordeum jubatum **87**
hornbeam *see Carpinus*
  betulus
Hosta **17**, *17*, *23*, *68*, **89**, 92, **93**,
  99, 118, *118*, *162*, *166*, **196**
  H. nakaiana *196*
  H. plantaginea **86**
  H. sieboldiana **73**, **89**, **93**
houseleek
  see Sempervivum
Houttuynia cordata
  'Chameleon' *131*
Hugens, Dick *155*

Humulus lupulus *115*
  H. l. 'Aureus' *115, 117*
Hydrangea 43, 81, **85**, *166*, **190**
  H. paniculata 'Grandiflora' *187*
  H. petiolaris 117
  H. 'Preziosa' *81*
  H. quercifolia **74**, **144**
  H. serrata **17**
Hypsela reniformis **95**
Hyssopus officinalis **196**
  H. o. subsp *aristatus* **103**

I

Ilex (holly) 45, **95**, *130*, *166*, **190**
  I. aquifolium
    I. a. 'Argentea Marginata'
      93
    I. a. 'Golden Queen' **92**
  I. crenata (Japanese holly)
    50, **51**
  I. x *meserveae* **92**
illusions 20–39
Impatiens 57, **165**
  hybrid *162*
Imperata cylindrica 92, **199**
  I. c. 'Rubra' *81*
In Goede Aarde *30*
insects *124, 127*
  infestations 133
inspection covers, hiding 35
Ipheion 59
Iris **17**, 59
  dwarf bearded **196**
  I. ensata *142*
  I. foetidissima **86**, **87**, 99, **196**
  I. laevigata *131*
  I. pallida 'Variegata' **93**
  I. pseudacorus *144*
  I. sibirica **69**, **86**, 87, **96**, *131*, *144*
  I. versicolor *131*
irrigation systems for
  containers *164*
Ishihara, Kazuyuki *133*
Itea ilicifolia 117
ivy *see Hedera*

J

Japanese evergreen azalea
  see Rhododendron
Japanese garden *30, 79*
Japanese holly *see*
  Ilex crenata
Japanese maple *see*
  Acer palmatum
Jasminum (jasmine) 36, **103**,
  113, *166*, **200**
  J. nudiflorum **200**
jungle-style planting 28
Juniperus scopulorum
  'Skyrocket' **96**, 99, **190**

K

kale *173*, **178**
  'Cavolo Nero' *178*
kerb stones 150
Kirengeshoma palmata **89**, 99,
  196, *196*
kiwi fruit *see Actinidia chinensis*
Kloet, Jacqueline van der *46,*
  62, 81, 87, 89, 90
Knautia
  K. arvensis **129**
  K. macedonica 55, **69**, *82*
Kniphofia **69**, **96**, **96**, *99*
  K. 'Little Maid' **196**
Koeleria glauca **93**, *199*
kohlrabi *174*, **178**
Koppen, Joke van 62
Kwekerij Van Nature *11, 13, 26,*
  29, 45

L

Lagurus ovatus **87**
Lamium maculatum 'Beacon
  Silver' 118
Landscape Agency, The *139*
Lantana *158*
large plants 79
Lathyrus odoratus (sweet pea)
  102, **103**, *117*
laurel, Portuguese *see*
  Prunus lusitanica
Laurus nobilis **95**, **117**, *166*, **190**
Lavandula **17**, **17**, 30, 53, **71**, 93,
  103, *140*, **192**
Lavatera x *clementii* **85**
lawns *11*, 12
  advantages 61
  disadvantages 61
layering with plants 40–75
  ground layer **62**, **65**, **75**
  middle layer **65**, **74**
  naturalistic 66–7
  three-layer principle 62
  upper layer **64**, **74**
leaf beets **175**, **178**, 180
leaf litter 45
leeks **175**, **178**
lemon verbena *185*
lettuce *174*, **178**
Leucanthemum vulgare **129**
Leucojum 59
Liatris spicata **17**
Libertia **96**, 99, **196**
light, garden aspect *14*
Ligularia dentata **92**
Ligustrum ovalifolium **92**, **93**, **190**
Lilium 59, **70**, **103**
  L. regale **103**
lime *see Tilia*
lime soil *see* alkaline soil
Limieten, De *162*
Limnanthes douglasii 56
Limonium platyphyllum **96**, 99,
  166, **196**
Linaria 69
  L. alpina **95**
Lindera benzoin **103**
linking house and garden 37, **38**
Linum 56
Liriodendron tulipifera
  (tulip tree) **49**
Liriope 55, **71**, **95**, 98, **101**, 118, **196**
  L. muscari 99
    L. m. 'Gold Band' **196**
Lobelia cardinalis **70**
logs *133, 133*
long thin garden
  see pipeline garden
Lonicera (honeysuckle) 36,
  103, *113*, 113, 114, *117*
  L. x *brownii* 'Dropmore
    Scarlet' *114*
  L. nitida (shrubby honeysuckle)
    50, **51**, **95**, **190**
  L. periclymenum *102*, **200**
love-in-a-mist *see Nigella*
Lunaria rediviva **86**, **87**, **196**, *196*
Lupinus 57, 66, **69**
Luzula (wood rush) **101**, 118
Lychnis coronaria *7*
Lysimachia punctata 55
Lythrum **96**, **99**, **196**
  L. salicaria **17**
    L. s. 'Robert' *96*

M

Macleaya cordata *169*
Magnolia grandiflora **113**
Mahonia **95**, 96
  M. x *media* 'Charity' **99**, **103**, **190**

Malus (crab apple/apple) 45, **48**, *64*, **74**, **86**, **87**, **188**
  M. x *robusta* 'Red Sentinel' 45
  M. tschonoskii **89**, **188**
Malva moschata 55
maple *see Acer*
marginal plants **127**
marigold *see Calendula; Tagetes*
marrows **175**
mass planting 28, **160–1**
Masterclasses
  how plants climb **112–13**
  how to layer with plants **64–5**
  plants' structure over time **98–9**
  sculpting with woody plants **48–51**
  top container design tips **160–1**
  two-season plants **86–7**
  types of fruit **176–7**
  types of vegetable **174–5**
Mathews, Yvonne *151*
Mathiasella bupleuroides **89**, **197**
Matteuccia 30
Maurières, Arnaud *59*
Maynard, Arne *144*
Mazus **95**
McKee, Jonathan *7*, *26*
McWilliam, Gavin *127*, *143*
meadow-style planting 28, 66, *133*
Meconopsis cambrica (Welsh poppy) *75*
Meijer, Willy *155*
Meneer Vermeer Tuinen *148*
Mentha **17**, **103**, **197**
  M. requienii **95**
Menyanthes trifoliata **131**
Merriments Gardens *53*
Mertensia **68**
mesh tunnel *183*
Mespilus germanica **89**, **188**
metal grids *147*
Milium effusum 'Aureum' *65*
mini-veg *178*
minimalism *27*
mirrors *22*
Miscanthus *53*, *70*, *74*
  M. 'Elfin' **101**
  M. sinensis **73**, **99**
    dwarf varieties **199**
    M. s. 'Gold Bar' **92**
    M. s. 'Gracillimus' *27*
    M. s. 'Gracillimus Nanus' **101**
    M. s. 'Little Kitten' **101**
    M. s. 'Little Zebra' **92**
    M. s. 'Morning Light' **93**
    M. s. 'Nippon' **101**
    M. s. 'Rigoletto' **93**
    M. s. 'Yakushima Dwarf'' *101*, *199*
    M. s. 'Zebrinus' **199**
Miss Willmott's ghost
  see Eryngium giganteum
moist soil in shady garden 45
Molinia 55, *81*
  M. caerulea **17**, **98**, **99**, **199**
    M. c. subsp. *arundinacea* *101*
Molopospermum peloponnesiacum *21*
Monarda **70**, **129**, **130**, **144**
mooli **178**, *179*
mulching *16*
Musa basjoo (banana) *11*, *79*, *105*, *169*
Muscari *59*, **201**
  M. armeniacum *201*
Myosotis sylvatica (forget-me-not) *57*, *157*

Myrtus communis **95**, **103**, *117*, **166**, **190**
mystery *see illusions*

N
Nandina domestica **95**, **190**
Narcissus (daffodil) 36, *59*, **68**, **201**
  'Cyclamineus' types **201**
  Jonquil types **103**, **201**
  N. 'Tête-à-tête' *20*
  Poeticus types **103**
  Tazetta types **103**, **201**
narrow gardens *13*
Nassella tenuissima
  see Stipa tenuissima
nasturtium *173*
native plants **129**
Nectaroscordum siculum *70*
Nemesia *56*, **82**
Nepeta (catmint) **17**, *54*, **69**, *82*, **166**
  N. x *faassenii* **17**, **197**, *197*
  N. 'Six Hills Giant' *7*
Nephrolepis exaltata *169*
Nigella **87**
  N. damascena (love-in-a-mist) *75*
niwaki *51*
Noble, Alexandra *140*
north-facing garden *14*
Norton, Mary *184–5*
nutrients, loss in soil from trees 44
Nymphaea (water lily) 36, **131**, *135*

O
oak *see Quercus*
Odiner, Erve *49*
O'Donoghue, Chris *151*
Oenothera **57**
Omphalodes **71**
onions **175**, *178*
Ophiopogon **95**, *118*, **196**
  O. planiscapus 'Nigrescens' *75*, **92**
Oriental greens *see stir-fry greens*
Origanum **17**, **69**, *129*
  O. vulgare **129**
ornament in garden *27*
Osmanthus **103**, **190**
  O. x *burkwoodii* **50**, *103*, **190**
Ossart, Eric *59*
Osteospermum **82**, **166**

P
pak choi **178**
palms *105*
Panicum virgatum **89**, **99**, **199**
  P. v. 'Shenandoah' **89**
pansy *see Viola*
Papaver (poppy) *75*
  annual *56*
  P. orientale (oriental poppy) **69**
  P. somniferum (opium poppy) *7*, **87**
parsley **180**
Parthenocissus **112**, *112*, *114*, *117*, *118*, **200**
  P. henryana *200*
  P. quinquefolia *53*, *200*
Passiflora (passion flower) **112**
  P. caerulea *115*, *185*
paths 28, 30, *31*, *31*, *33*, *75*, *139*, *142*, *150*
patios *13*
  doors *37*, *37*
  fruit for **176**
Paulownia **49**
  P. tomentosa **48**
pavers *147*, *150*

paving 25, 26, 27, 33, **38**, *38*, **135**, *147*, *147*
  circular 28
paving stones *150*
peach *see Prunus*
pears *7*, **176**
Pearson, Dan *125*
Pearson, Philippa *145*
peas **174**, *178*, **180**
Pelargonium *57*, **165**
  P. crispum *169*
Pennisetum 55, **69**, *101*
  P. alopecuroides 66, *87*, **99**, **199**
Penstemon **82**, **129**, *166*, **197**
  P. 'Rich Ruby' **96**
perennials **193–8**
  autumn colour **89**
  clump-forming **69**
  colourful foliage **92–3**
  combinations 66
  for containers **166**
  early foliage **89**
  elegant foliage **89**
  evergreen 55, **94**, **95**
  foliage types **68**
  grown as annuals 57
  herbaceous *54–5*
  large leaves **89**
  late-flowering 85, **85**
  late half-hardy **82**
  long-flowering 82, *82*
  long-lived clump-forming 54
  long-lived running 55
  long-lived static 54
  narrow **70**
  repeat-flowering **82**
  seasonal performances **80**, **86**
  for seed heads **87**
  short-lived 55
  structural plants **96**
  for swales **144**
  upright **82**
  weak-stemmed **69**
Perkins, Nicky *79*
Perovskia
  P. atriplicifolia **17**, **99**, **192**, **197**
  P. 'Blue Spire' **128**, *187*, **192**
Persian speedwell
  see Veronica persica
Persicaria **69**, *81*
  P. affinis **71**
  P. amplexicaulis **70**, **82**, **99**
perspective in garden *32–3*, **90**
pests
  protection from *183*
  resistant plants *179*
Petunia *57*, **165**
Phacelia tanacetifolia **87**
Philadelphus
  P. 'Belle Etoile' **190**
  P. coronarius 'Aureus' **92**, **190**
Phillyrea **51**
Phlomis **193**
  P. russeliana **68**, **86**, **87**, **95**, **99**, **130**, **197**
Phlox **70**, *129*
  P. divaricata *142*
  P. paniculata **197**
    P. p. 'Norah Leigh' **93**
  P. subulata *158*
Phormium 'Jester' 36
Photinia **48**, *92*
  P. x *fraseri* **190**
Phygelius **85**, **197**
  P. x *rectus* 'African Queen' **197**
Physocarpus opulifolius **144**, **190**
  P. o. 'Diabolo' **92**
Picea mariana 'Nana' **95**
Pieris **17**, **92**, **95**, **190**
  P. japonica 'Katsura' *162*
Pileostegia viburnoides *117*

pioneer species of trees 45
pipeline garden 23, 25
Pittosporum **166**
  P. tenuifolium **95**, **191**
    P. t. 'Irene Paterson' *46*
    P. t. 'Variegatum' **50**
plant choices for small gardens *76–107*
planting combinations 43, **66**, **160–1**
Platanus **48**
play *61*
pleaching *38*, **48**
plums *176*
Poa labillardieri **93**
poles in garden *34*, *34*, *135*
pollarding **48**
pollination *129*
Polygonatum **96**, **99**, **197**
  P. curvistylum **197**
Polystichum setiferum **99**
pools 25, 28, 33, 36, *127*, *135*, *139*
  creating **127**
  edges **127**
poppy
  opium poppy *see Papaver somniferum*
  oriental poppy *see Papaver orientale*
  Welsh poppy *see Meconopsis cambrica*
Portuguese laurel
  see Prunus lusitanica
Postma, Tom *123*, *127*
potash fertilisers **165**
potatoes **175**
Potentilla **69**
  P. alba **95**
  P. aurea **95**
  P. fruticosa **85**, *162*, **193**
pots *see containers*
prairies 66
Pratia **95**
Preston, Carrie *134–5*
Primula **68**, **166**
  P. elatior **197**, *197*
  P. florindae **144**, **197**
  P. japonica *142*
  P. vulgaris **197**
  polyanthus varieties **197**
protecting vegetables *182–3*
Prunella **95**
  P. vulgaris (selfheal) **129**, **131**
pruning *see coppicing; pollarding*
Prunus 45, *113*, **188**
  P. avium **130**
  P. cerasifera (ornamental cherry)
    P. c. 'Nigra' **92**, **188**
    P. c. 'Pissardii' *33*, *79*
  P. x *cistena* **92**, **188**
  P. lusitanica (Portuguese laurel) **50**, *50*, **95**, **191**
  P. sargentii **89**
  P. serrula **89**
  P. 'Shogetsu' **188**
  P. 'Ukon' **86**
Pterocarya **49**
Pulmonaria 55, **68**, **86**, **93**, **197**
Pulsatilla vulgaris **17**, **87**, **98**, **197**
pumpkins **175**
Putnam, Steve 35
Pyracantha **87**, **95**, *113*, *113*, **191**
  P. 'Navaho' **191**
Pyrus salicifolia 'Pendula' **93**, **188**

Q
Quercus (oak) 45, **49**
  Q. ilex **48**
Quirke, Paul *139*

R

radish **180**
rain 141
   collecting rain water 145
   planning a mini-rain garden
      142–4
raised beds 30, 30, 173, **181**, 185
raspberries **177**
rectangular garden 13
recycling 139, 148–51, 155
redcurrants 177
Rhamnus alaternus
   'Argenteovariegata' **93**, **191**
Rheum 89
   R. palmatum **73**
Rhodiola **158**
Rhododendron 17, **17**, **95**, **103**,
   123, **166**, **191**
   deciduous azalea **191**
   Japanese azalea **50**, **191**
   R. 'Freya' **191**
   R. 'Victorine Hefting'
      (azalea) 46
Rhus typhina **89**, **188**
Ribes
   R. odoratum **89**
   R. sanguineum **129**, **191**
Ricinus communis (castor oil
   plant) 105, 169, 169
Ridder, Maayke de 43
Robinia pseudoacacia 'Frisia'
   73, 74
Rodgersia 68, **89**, **92**, **99**, 105, **197**
roof garden 11, 35, 35, 45, 139,
   140, 141
   containers for 155
root vegetables **174**, 175
rootstocks 176
Rosa 87, **130**, **191**
   climbing 53, 62, **113**, 115
   'English Rose' class **103**
   ramblers **113**, 123
   for scent 36
   R. 'Blushing Lucy' 53
   R. 'Bobbie James' 111
   R. 'Climbing Iceberg' 115
   R. 'Fru Dagmar Hastrup' **86**
   R. 'Handel' 53
   R. 'Zéphirine Drouhin' **191**
Rosier, Hans 155
Rosmarinus officinalis **71**, 94,
   95, **99**, **103**, **166**, **193**
routes around garden 22, 23
Rowe, Charlotte 147
Rudbeckia 54, **69**, 169, 169
   R. fulgida **85**, **197**
runner beans **174**, **180**, **185**
rush, wood *see Luzula*
Ruta graveolens **93**, **166**, **193**

S

salad leaf crops 35, **174**, **180**
Salix (willow) **17**, **48**, **135**, **144**
   dwarf **193**
   pollarding **48**
   S. alba **49**
   S. exigua **93**
   S. fargesii **49**
   S. lanata **93**, **191**
   S. magnifica **49**
   S. repens var *argentea* **93**
salvage style 148
Salvia **69**, **82**, **103**, **166**
   S. guarantica 'Blue Enigma' 82
   S. x jamensis 'Hot Lips' **197**
   S. microphylla **197**
   S. nemorosa **17**, **82**, **130**, **198**
      S. n. 'Caradonna' 101
   S. officinalis **71**, **93**
      S. o. 'Icterina' **92**
      S. o. 'Purpurascens' **92**

S. x superba **17**, **82**, **198**
S. x sylvestris **17**, **82**, **198**
S. uliginosa **85**
Sambucus (elder) 49
sandy soil 16
Sanguisorba **17**, **69**, **89**, **99**, **144**, **198**
   S. officinalis **198**
   S. tenuifolia 'White Tanna' 96
Santolina chamaecyparissus
   71, **90**, **93**, **193**
   S. c. 'Nana' **193**
Sarcococca **191**
Sassafras albidum **89**
Satureja **103**
   S. montana **198**
Saxifraga **166**
   S. fortunei **68**, **85**, **198**
Scabiosa stellata **87**
scarlet pimpernel *see*
   Anagallis arvensis
scent in garden 36, 102–3
Schefflera 105
Schisandra **87**, **200**
   S. grandiflora 117
Schizachyrium scoparium **89**,
   199
Schizanthus 56
Scilla 59, **68**, **201**
Scleranthus **158**
screens 22, 23, 28, 35
sculpture 27, 28, 31, 31, **38**
seasonal plants 80
   structure and 96–7, **98–9**
   see also under specific
      plants, e.g. perennials
seating 21, 33, 35, **38**, 105, 123,
   135
sedges *see Carex*
Sedum 35, 35, **69**, **87**, **95**, 133,
   151, **158**, **166**
   S. 'Herbstfreude' 30
   S. 'Matrona' **37**, 198
   S. spectabile **17**, 54, **85**, **99**, **198**
   S. telephium **92**, **99**, **198**
seed heads **80**, **86–7**, **87**, **130**
   grasses 101
   seasonal performances 86
selfheal *see Prunella vulgaris*
Selinum **89**
   S. wallichianum **99**, **198**
Sempervivum (houseleek)
   133, **158**, *158*
Senecio ovatus **129**
sensory garden 36
Sesleria **17**, 55, **101**, **200**
Setaria italica 'Red Jewel' 169
shady garden **14**, 14
   shade-tolerant plants 45
   from trees 44
   vegetables for **180**
shakkei 25
shallow gardens 13
shape of garden 13
Sharkey, Susan 117, 139
sheds 11, 35, 150
shelter provision for wildlife **125**
shelving **158**
shrubs **188–92**
   autumn colour **89**
   for colourful foliage **92–3**
   for colourful fruit **87**
   for containers **166**
   evergreen **95**
   for hedging **50**
   late-flowering **85**, 85
   layering **191**
   sculpting **48–51**
   seasonal performances **80**, **86**
   spring-flowering 82
   for swales **144**
   value of 46–7

for walls **113**
   see also sub-shrubs
Silene dioica **129**
simplicity 27
Sisyrinchium **166**
size, illusions 22, 25, 38
Skimmia **166**
   S. japonica **95**, **191**
      S. j. 'Thereza' **191**
Smith, Stephen 7, 26
smoke bush
   see Cotinus coggygria
Smyrnium perfoliatum 62
snowdrop *see Galanthus*
soak-aways 140, **145**
soil
   checking acidity 16
   for climbers 114
   cob 151
   for containers 162
   improving 16
   preparation for fruit and
      vegetables 181
   types 16
Solidago **70**, **129**, **130**, **144**
   S. caesia **129**
Sorbus (rowan) **87**, **89**, **135**, **188**
sound in garden 36
south-facing garden 14, 14
Southend-on-Sea Borough
   Council 124
space
   assessment 8–19
   dividing up 21
   filling 28–9
Special Trees 155
speedwell, Persian
   see Veronica persica
spinach **178**, **180**
Spiraea japonica
   S. 'Golden Princess' **92**, **191**
   S. 'Goldflame' **92**, **191**
Sporobolus heterolepis **69**, **99**,
   101, **200**
spreading plants for containers
   161
spurge *see Euphorbia*
   petty *see Euphorbia peplus*
squashes **175**
Stachys byzantina 'Big Ears' 90
Stam, Erwin 61, 167
stepping stones 151
steps 30, **38**
Stewart, James 35, **38**
Stewartia 89, **188**
Steyaert, Floris 151
Stipa 55
   S. calamagrostis 53, **101**, **200**
   S. gigantea **99**, **101**, **200**
   S. tenuissima **27**, 55, **69**, **99**,
      101, **200**
stir-fry greens **174**, **178**, **180**
Stone, Paul 173
storage space 35
strawberries 164, **177**
strawberry tree
   see Arbutus unedo
structural plants 44–53, 96–7, **160–1**
   perennial **96**
   seasons and **98–9**
   woody **96**
sub-gardens 25
sub-shrubs 52–3, **71**, **192–3**
   for colourful foliage **92**
   evergreen 94, **95**
Succisa pratensis **129**
succulents **161**
   see also specific types
sustainable spaces 136–57
Swagerman, Lumine 43, 82
swales 140, 141, 142, 143

plants for **144**
sweet corn **175**
sweet peas *see Lathyrus odoratus*
sweet William 57
Swiss chard 173, **175**, *175*, 178
Symphyotrichum **129**
   S. lateriflorum var.
      horizontalis **85**
Symphytum **129**
   S. x uplandicum 'Axminster
      Gold' **92**, **198**
Syringa
   S. meyeri **166**, **191**
   S. pubescens subsp
      microphylla 'Superba' 191

T

Tagetes (marigold) 56, 105, *179*
Talsma, Jan 158
Taxus baccata (yew) **48**, **50**,
   51, **130**
   T. b. 'Standishii' **95**
   T. b. Fastigiata Aurea Group 14
tayberries **177**
terraces **38**, 107
Teucrium
   T. chamaedrys **71**, **191**
   T. fruticans **95**
Thalictrum **70**, 81, **89**, **96**, **99**,
   133, **198**
Thompson, Elspeth 111, 114, 117, 124
Thuja occidentalis 'Rheingold' **95**
Thujopsis dolabrata 45
Thymus **17**, **71**, **95**, 151
Tiarella **129**
   T. cordifolia 142
Tilia (lime) 49
   pleached **38**, **48**, 49
tiling 25
timbers, recycled 148, 150, 151
Timmermans, Gerda **135**
Timmermans, Willem 123, 127
toads 127
tomatoes 157, **175**, *175*, 185
topiary 34, 51, **51**, 65, 81
   plants for **51**
touching plants 36
Traas, Jan and Addy 53
Trachelospermum **103**, **117**
   T. asiaticum **200**
   T. jasminoides 36, **95**, 117, **166**,
      200
trailing plants 118
transpiration 141
tree fern *see Dicksonia antarctica*
tree fruit 176
trees 13, 25, 29, **188**
   autumn colour **89**
   for colourful foliage **92–3**
   for colourful fruit **87**
   for containers **166**
   disadvantages 44
   for hedging **50**
   pioneer 45
   sculpting **48–51**
   seasonal performances **86**
   for upper layer **64**
   for wildlife 133
trellis 22, 35, **185**
Tricyrtis **85**, **198**
   T. 'Shimone' **198**
Trifolium (clover) **131**
   T. pratense **129**
Trollius **17**, **144**
tropical planting
   see exotic planting
troughs 143
tubers for tropical look 105
tulip tree
   see Liriodendron tulipifera

Tulipa 59, 65, **201**
  T. Darwin Group **201**
  T. Kaufmanniana Group **201**
  T. 'Orange Emperor' 59
turnips 178
Typha minima **131**

U
Uncina rubra **92**, **101**, **200**
unity in design **27**
urbanite 150

V
Vaccinium **17**
Valeriana officinalis **70**
van Sweden, James 79
variegated foliage **50**, 90
vegetables 170–85
  in containers *157, 180, 183*
  growing 178–9
  protection 182–3
  requirements 180–1
  soil for 16
  types **174–5**
Veratrum 89
Verbascum **57**, **198**
  V. bombyciferum **99**
  V. nigrum **86**, **87**, **99**

Verbena 56
  V. bonariensis **70**, 79, **82**, **99**, **129**, **130**, *187*, **198**
Veronica **71**, **166**
  V. austriaca **17**
  V. persica (Persian speedwell) **131**
  V. prostrata **158**
Veronicastrum **96**, **198**
  V. virginicum 54, **70**, **144**
Versluis, Emiel *148*
vertical focal points 34
vertical space 12
  planting up 108–19
Viburnum **144**, **166**
  V. x *bodnantense* **191**
  V. x *burkwoodii* **103**
  V. x *carlcephalum* **103**, **191**
  V. davidii **95**, **192**, *192*
  V. opulus **86**, **87**, **130**, *135*
  V. plicatum 'Watanabe' *81*
  V. tinus **95**, **192**
Vinca **95**, **99**
  V. minor **198**, *198*
    V. m. 'Argenteovariegata' **92**
vine, grape *111*
vine, Japanese ornamental see *Vitis coignetiae*

Viner, Spencer 36
Viola (pansy) 57, **68**, *157, 158*
  V. cornuta 71, **82**, **198**
  V. odorata **103**
Virginia creeper
  see *Parthenocissus*
Vissers, Ton *118*, **161**
Vitis (ornamental vine) **112**, **117**, *117*, *135*
  V. coignetiae 111, *114*

W
walkways see paths
wallflower see *Erysimum*
walls 150
  aspect 114
  colour 27
  drystone 133, *133*
  earth **151**
water
  management 139, 141
  provision for wildlife 126–7
  run-off 139, *140*, 141, 142, *143*
  storage 141
  table 141
water butts 145, *145*
water features 28, 33, 36, **38**
water lily see *Nymphaea*

watering systems for containers 164
Wayne Amiel Garden 79
weeds, benign **131**
west-facing garden 14
Whitehead, Carol **184–5**
Whiten, Geoffrey 162
wild gardens 66
wildlife, gardens for 120–35, *185*
  planting up 128–9
willow see *Salix*
Wilson, Andrew 127, *143*
winter interest plants **86**
Wisteria *111*, 111, **113**, *115*, **117**
  W. sinensis *185*
Witte, Tom de *13*, *21*, *22*, *27*
woodland
  edging 43
  layering with plants 43
  shade-tolerant plants 45
woodpiles 133

Y
yew see *Taxus*
Yucca 105, **166**, **192**
  Y. filamentosa 98, **99**

Z
Zimmer, Johnny **38**
Zinnia 56

Acknowledgements

This book would not have been possible without the help and cooperation of many garden owners who have generously allowed their gardens to be photographed. The following garden makers were specifically interviewed for the project, or we made extensive use of their gardens for the images: Wayne Amiel, David Cund & Sally Golding, Elsa Day, Clare Dryhurst, Hermione Frankel, Mark Gandy, Jonathan McKee, Willy Meijer & Hans Rosier, Mary Norton, Madelon Oostwoud, Nicky Perkins, Ton Ploegmakers, James Stewart, Gerda Timmermans.

In addition, we would like to thank the following designers whose small gardens inspired us: Joanne Bernstein, Joost Willems & Jan van Opstal of de Heerenhof, Jacqueline van der Kloet of de Theetuin, Stephen Smith, Erwin Stam, Lumine Swagerman, Ruud Vermeer of Meneer Vermeer Tuinen, Spencer Viner, Frank Heijligers, Frank van der Linden, Annie Guilfoyle, and Tom de Witte.

We have also used pictures taken in gardens by Maayke at some stage in the past, and are very grateful to owners and designers for their permission to use these images: Louise van den Akker, Erna Aupers, Anne Brown, Paul Cox, Catherine Cuyckens, Nicolien van Dam, Hof ter Dieren, Helen Dillon, Stella Faber, Erik Jan van Geijn, Leen Goedegebuure, Lydia Gunning, Klazina van Kippersluis, Petra Koetsier, Tessa Kraus & Paola Welsch, de Limieten, Jonathan McKee Mandenmakers family, Mariëtte Masson, Piet Mosch, Odette van Mourik, Henk and Ina Nan,

Nooren-Smeets family, Erve Odinck, Cilia Prenen, Lumine van Raaijen family, Lumine Swagerman, Willem Timmermans & Tom Postma, Frank Thuyls, Jan & Addy Traas, Régine Vanherle-Vuylsteke, Frank Wilson, and Karel Zwaan.

Some of the gardens mentioned above have been professionally designed, and we have also included a few show gardens. We are grateful for the good work of: Chris Beardshaw, Marianne Blaauwboer, Tom Brekelmans, Lesley Bremness, Kristof van den Bouwhuysen, Chetwood and Patrick Collins, Teresa Davies, Arnaud Maurières & Eric Ossart, Sophie von Maltzan, Arne Maynard, Merriments Gardens, Alexandra Noble, Chris O'Donoghue, Nigel Dunnett, Judith Glover, Neil Goldsmith & Sabina Edwards, Kate Gould, Hadlow College, Adrian Hallam, Mike Harvey, Darren Hawkes, Samantha Hawkins, Luke Heydon, Rita Higgins & Paul Quirke, In Goede Aarde, Kazuyuki Ishihara, Jacques van Leuken, Yvonne Mathews, Charlotte Rowe, Dan Pearson, Philippa Pearson, Steve Putnam, Susan Sharkey, Paul Stone, Ton Vissers, Andrew Wilson & Gavin McWilliam, Nick Williams-Ellis, and Geoffrey Whiten.

Finally, we wish to thank Helen Griffin and the team at Frances Lincoln publishers for commissioning the book and seeing it through to print, to Zia Allaway for her editorial work and Becky Clarke for the design.

Noel Kingsbury
Maayke de Ridder

GARY PUBLIC LIBRARY

712.6 K 2016
Kingsbury, Noel,
New small garden

GARY PUBLIC LIBRARY

3 9222 03182 8325